THE
Poetic World
—— OF ——
Emily Brontë

To my inspiration and teacher,
Professor Billie Jo Inman, Ph.D. in English
The University of Texas 1962
Professor Emerita, The University of Arizona 1963 to1994

THE
Poetic World
— O F —
Emily Brontë

Poems from the Author of
Wuthering Heights

LAURA INMAN

sussex
ACADEMIC
PRESS
Brighton • Chicago • Toronto

Copyright © Laura Inman, 2014.

The right of Laura Inman to be identified as author of this work has been
asserted in accordance with the Copyright, Designs and Patents Act 1988.

2 4 6 8 10 9 7 5 3 1

First published in 2014 in Great Britain by
SUSSEX ACADEMIC PRESS
PO Box 139
Eastbourne BN24 9BP

and in the United States of America by
SUSSEX ACADEMIC PRESS
Independent Publishers Group
814 N. Franklin Street, Chicago, IL 60610

and in Canada by
SUSSEX ACADEMIC PRESS (CANADA)
1108 / 115 Antibes Drive, Toronto, Ontario M2R 2Y9

British Library Cataloguing in Publication Data
A CIP catalogue record for this book is available from the British Library.

Library of Congress Cataloging-in-Publication Data
Brontë, Charlotte, 1816–1855.
[Poems. Selections]
The Poetic World of Emily Brontë : Poems From the Author of
Wuthering Heights / [edited by] Laura Inman.
pages   cm
Includes bibliographical references and index.
ISBN 978-1-84519-645-5 (pb : alk. paper)
I. Inman, Laura. II. Title.
PR4166.I56 2014
821'.8—dc23

2014005775

Typeset & designed by Sussex Academic Press, Brighton & Eastbourne.
Printed TJ International, Padstow, Cornwall.

Contents

CONTENTS

Introduction

Emily Brontë is best known, perhaps solely known, as a novelist, the author of one of the all-time great works, *Wuthering Heights*. Readers for generations have paused at Lockwood's final words at the graves of Catherine, Edgar, and Heathcliff, with the wistful feeling that accompanies the end, eager to read something else that Emily Brontë wrote. At that point, one might discover that she was a poet because there is almost nothing else by her to read except her poetry, no other works of fiction or letters. Luckily, her poems fill the void.

After discovering that Brontë was a poet, one can approach her poetry, in the typical way, by reading a few poems at random. Although she is undeservedly marginalized as a poet, there are editions of her poems available. The definitive collection of Brontë's poems is *The Complete Poems of Emily Jane Brontë*, by C.W. Hatfield. It serves as a valuable companion for scholars, as all of her poems, even incomplete ones and fragments, are presented in chronological order, without the editing by Charlotte Brontë and others that occurred after Brontë's death. However, perusing single poems will not acquaint the reader with Brontë's poetic work and her life as this book intends to do. First, the poems might pose some difficulties for the uninitiated. Mostly lacking in titles and at times arcane and archaic in diction, her poetry becomes more accessible when read with the explanations and interpretations paired with each poem in this book. Also, having a context for a poem aids in one's understanding of it. Here, selections from her poetic work are arranged according to thematic topics: nature; mutability; love; death; captivity and freedom; hope and despair;

imagination; and spirituality. For each topic, I have given biographical, historical, and literary context, including connections to *Wuthering Heights*. The topical arrangement compensates for the lack of a title and the contextual discussion primes the reader to grasp and appreciate the meaning of the poems in that chapter. Regarding the biographical context in particular, not only does a biographical context for a poem help clarify its meaning, the reverse holds true: one can gain otherwise unknowable information about Brontë's personality and views from her poems. Because biography figures so importantly in this dual role, I have started this book with a general outline of Brontë's life and have added to the facts my deductions about certain personality traits and beliefs relevant to a better understanding of her poetry. Also, throughout the book, I make connections among her life, her poetry, and her novel as well. Indeed, all three — the identity of the poet, the poems, and *Wuthering Heights* — coalesce into Brontë's poetic world. Given that the whole is a sum of the sequential chapters, this book is best read by turning the pages in order. Although the usual edition of poetry does not demand reading from beginning to end, it is a distinguishing feature of this book of poetry that it should be read initially in that manner because there is a thematic progression to the presentation of the poems: ideas in the poems connect and often build upon preceding notions, as do my discussions about the poems.

There are two points of clarification that pertain to the presentation of the poems. First, as mentioned above, most of Brontë's poems do not have titles, so I have identified them by their first lines, even those few that do have a title. The lack of titles is unusual, but not unprecedented; for example, Shakespeare's sonnets do not have titles. Second, any one-time curious word-usage or archaism is explained when it appears in a poem. However, the following frequently appear. "Brow" can be read to mean "forehead," but in other instances suggests the entire face. The predilection for that word seems to be its ease for rhyming. The word "below" appears many times, such as in the lines, "We part below to meet on high." It is a shorthand way of saying on earth as opposed to in heaven. The word "beneath" is at times used in that same way. Also designating human existence on earth is the word "clay," as in the lines, "Alas! the countless links are strong / that bind us to our clay." Brontë typically uses the archaic "thee," "thou," "thy," and "thine," which she would not have used in speaking. The use of those pronouns for the modern "you" and "yours" was poetic convention and also would have facilitated rhyming.

One should read and consider the poems several times. Like all great art, they improve on better acquaintance. Then, once her poems become familiar, one can come back to them again and again because poems are for perpetual reading, like a spiritual source. Brontë's poetry depicts a world of sensations and sentiments, some familiar and others peculiar, expressed in lyrical lines that linger — and it continues our relationship with Emily Brontë after concluding *Wuthering Heights*.

CHAPTER ONE

Emily Brontë, the Poet and the Person

Knowing about Emily Brontë adds to or even creates an interest in her poetry because she was a fascinating person: an independent spirit, a forward thinker, and a literary genius. Further, a familiarity with the poet rounds out the poetry-reading experience, particularly when reading a body of work, rather than a few random poems, because poetry, more than prose, is a personal matter. It invites the reader to feel a rapport with the poet, who can become a compatriot and sharer of sentiments.

Emily Jane Brontë lived for twenty-nine years, from 1818 to 1848, which period saw the close of the Romantic era and included the early Victorian era. Her father, the Reverend Patrick Brontë, extremely intelligent, caring, and hardworking, was ordained into the Church of England and held the perpetual curacy of Haworth, having risen from the poverty of his boyhood in Ireland to become an English gentleman — although a poor one. Her mother, Maria, died when Emily was three, leaving six children: Maria, Elizabeth, Charlotte, Branwell, Emily and Anne. Her two oldest sisters died in 1825, at the ages of eleven and ten after a disastrous stay at Cowan Bridge School, a boarding institution for the daughters of poor clergymen, which turned out to be a harsh, cold, and unhealthy place. Cowan Bridge was the inspiration for Lowood School in Charlotte Brontë's *Jane Eyre*. Charlotte and Emily were also there at the time their sisters became ill; Emily, at five, being the youngest student on the premises. Tuberculosis caused the deaths of Maria and Elizabeth and eventually claimed Emily and Anne, who died within five months of each other. It also most likely contributed to Branwell's death, three months before Emily died, and Charlotte's, in 1855. Mr. Brontë lived to the age of eighty-four.

Except for a very few brief periods when Emily was away at a boarding school, as a student or teacher, she was at the parsonage, her beloved home, situated at the edge of Haworth, England, and a stone's throw across a crowded cemetery from her father's church. The back door of the two-story brick parsonage opened onto the moors — a seemingly endless expanse of low hills and valleys, scarce of trees, with low stone walls following the contours of the heath. In a poem "A little while, a little while" Brontë describes how well she knew the landscape of the moors: "That was the scene; I knew it well, / I knew the path-ways far and near, / That, winding o'er each billowy swell / Marked out the tracks of wandering deer." She also reproduces the moors in the description of the land lying between Thrushcross Grange and Wuthering Heights. Her home, the Brontë Parsonage, still stands today, maintained by the Brontë Society, with rooms of Brontë artifacts — a place well-worth visiting.

When Charlotte, Emily, and Anne were grown, young women, the necessity of making a living preyed upon them. Once their father died, they would be without a home. There was no annuity or savings; Mr. Brontë, although frugal, had never had sufficient means to do more than survive. It might be difficult for the modern mind to imagine the lack of opportunity that shackled the Victorian woman. Particularly for a "lady," which Emily would have been considered since her father was a clergyman, there were no paths to pursue except marriage, living as a dependent on a family member, or teaching, whether as a governess or in a boarding school. These choices were grim for Charlotte, Emily, and Anne. None of the three seemed likely to marry. Indeed, none of the Brontë children did marry, except Charlotte, but her marriage ended with her death after only nine months. Branwell was not going to support his sisters; his attempts at various careers ended in failure. Charlotte and Anne had tried to accept the fate of a governess, although with the utmost hatred; but Emily could not bear to be away from home, much less interact with strangers in the subservient role of governess. The three sisters would attempt at one point to operate their own school in the parsonage, but would not receive a single expression of interest. They also were not suited to follow the path of women who immigrated, where in the comparative freedom and opportunity of Australia or America they might better make their own way, such as by owning a shop.

As the question of their financial future grew desperate, one surprising twist to the plot of their lives occurred. Their aunt, who had lived at the parsonage since the time of Mrs. Brontë's death, left, upon her death, a small sum to Charlotte, Emily, and Anne. It was an astonishing development, and although the sum was not enough to live on for long, it did give the three sisters the funds to publish a volume of their poems in 1846, using their pseudonyms for the first time: Currer Bell, Ellis Bell, and Acton Bell. One reviewer noted the beauty of Ellis Bell's lyrical voice, and Charlotte and Anne acknowledged Emily as the most gifted poet among them. Despite the merit of Emily's poems, the volume went unnoticed, selling only three copies. Poetry was the family hobby. Mr. Brontë had written and had published some poems, many of a religious nature, and he also would include a clever and thoughtful poem in a letter. Charlotte and Anne, as noted, had poems handy to contribute when Charlotte discovered Emily's poems one day and promoted the idea of the volume containing the work of all three sisters. Branwell yearned to be a poet, but he met with no success in any of his endeavors, owing in large part to his addiction to alcohol and opium. His presence in the parsonage, frequently raving drunk and in debt, created great unhappiness and tension.

After the failure of the volume of poetry, the legacy left by their aunt also allowed them to attempt to become novelists and be free, at least for a while, of the dreaded prospect of serving as governesses. Poetry and theater were male bastions, but the novel was fairly new to the time, and women such as Anne Radcliff, Mary Shelley, and Jane Austen had successfully exploited the opportunity. Every night after Mr. Brontë went to bed at nine o'clock, the three sisters gathered at the table in the parlor. With ink wells, nib-tipped pens, and reams of paper they wrote their lengthy novels by the firelight from the grate and the glow of candles and took turns reading aloud their work. At the end of 1847, Emily's *Wuthering Heights* and Anne's *Agnes Grey* appeared in print together as a three-volume set. Emily and Anne, after numerous rejections by publishers, had paid a large sum of money to publish their novels, greatly diminishing their meager legacy. Charlotte's first novel, *The Professor*, was not accepted for publication even at her own expense, and she had turned her attention to writing her second novel, *Jane Eyre*. It appeared even before her sisters' novels because Charlotte's publisher was far more reputable and productive than Emily's and Anne's. *Jane Eyre* was a great success, and the financial worries would have been allayed; however, one can wonder how much that mitigated for Emily the failure of *Wuthering Heights*, as unappreciated as her poetry had been. Her sisters, critics, and the public disliked and, apparently, failed to understand it. Charlotte kept trying to justify or explain it in the years between Emily's death and her own. A year after its publication, Emily died and was laid to rest in Haworth Church under the stone slab that covered the family burial vault. Posthumous interest in *Wuthering Heights* arose in the slip-stream of *Jane Eyre* and Charlotte's notoriety.

To investigate Brontë's life beyond the bare facts and to explore her thoughts and personality, biographers must deduce and surmise because there is a surprising lack of information about her. In an era notable for letter writers, she wrote only a couple of notes to her sister Anne and a few brief lines once to a friend of Charlotte and she did not keep a diary. Essays that she wrote in French, while studying at the Pensionnat Heger in Brussels, are extant and do offer some glimpses into her ideas and personality. In particular, her essay "The Palace of Death" reveals her view on alcoholism, which surfaces in *Wuthering Heights* in the character of Hindley Earnshaw. I have translated and included that essay in the Appendix.

Not only is there a dearth of her own writing, but reports and anecdotes about her are rare because she had almost no acquaintances outside of her family. The few who had met her never knew her well because she kept to herself, and, of course, they would not have known at the time that she would be worth remembering. The source for much of the information about Emily comes from Charlotte, who wrote letters, knew and conversed with people, became a person of renown before her death and a subject of biography shortly after. Yet, the more I have learned about Charlotte, the less I trust her view of Emily. Charlotte and Emily had very different natures, and there is reason to believe that they did not see eye to eye on many things, despite the fact that all three sisters were very close.

Biographers come up short particularly in recounting Emily's thoughts and plans during the last year of her life, the period after the poor reception of *Wuthering Heights*, and are given to speculating about her in various and dubious ways. The main source of information about her, Charlotte's correspondence, falls silent until the onset of the tuberculosis that would cause Emily's death within two months of the first symptoms. At that point Charlotte becomes voluble on Emily's suffering and her refusal to seek medical care. Emily's adamant refusal is well known as revealing something about her character; however, not calling a doctor was not unusual. No doctor was present at Branwell's demise. It was estimated that approximately twenty-two percent of the deaths at the time in Haworth occurred without the presence of a doctor.[1] Mr. Brontë kept a medical guide book handy for home self-help. On the other hand, Mr. Brontë did consult doctors. He even had surgery on his eyes, which amazingly was effective to remove his cataracts. Charlotte thought that medical attention would be beneficial for Emily. Anne, who fell ill also of tuberculosis shortly after Emily died, would actively seek medical care and follow all available regimes — to no avail. Emily was prescient in refusing

---

[1] Ann Dinsdale, *The Brontës at Haworth* (London: Frances Lincoln Ltd, 2006), 120.

medical care because she knew, I believe, that doctors were best avoided. They could do nothing at that time to treat tuberculosis or alleviate the symptoms, and the diets and bloodletting they prescribed were more harmful than beneficial. Albeit from the enlightened viewpoint of the present age, it does seem that calling a doctor for tuberculosis was an act of nearly superstitious desperation, and Emily was not that kind of person. The scourge of tuberculosis, called consumption at the time, and how it attacked families and great poets, might be of interest, so I have noted in the Bibliography sources of information on its pathology and progression. Just as Mr. Brontë knew that Anne's transition to the milder climate of Scarborough and consulting doctors would not save her, Emily knew that a doctor could offer no help. She had described in *Wuthering Heights* three cases of tuberculosis in realistic medical detail, all ending in death — those of Francis Earnshaw, Edgar Linton, and Linton Heathcliff. Also regarding why she refused medical treatment, I have to think that she generally held doctors, if not in low regard, at least as ineffectual to do anything much other than deliver bad news, given her depiction of Dr. Kenneth in *Wuthering Heights*. Dr. Kenneth bluntly tells Hindley that his wife. Francis, will not last long and he shows up to tell Nelly the news of Hindley's death. He is summoned to attend Mr. Earnshaw after he has died, just to confirm that he is indeed dead, and he has a record of not shortening the illness or saving the life of a single patient whom he attends throughout the story.

One is left to wonder and surmise about the last year of her life and her thoughts upon the failure of *Wuthering Heights*. The facts suggest that she was dismayed or even jaded about publishing. Charlotte and Anne took up a second novel promptly at the lack of success of their first. After Charlotte's first novel, *The Professor*, was not accepted for publication under any terms, she rather promptly wrote *Jane Eyre*, and Anne turned her attention from a flagging *Agnes Grey* to write *The Tenant of Wildfell Hall*. There is only speculation that Emily had started another novel at the time of her death, and it is likely that she had not. Perhaps she was too attached to *Wuthering Heights* to write another, or she might have been disgusted with the experience of rejection. In any event, "failure" did seem to affect her differently than it did her sisters. However, neither her novel's poor reception nor the failure of the volume of poetry kept her from writing poetry. She continued writing it up to her final illness, from which one easily concludes the importance of poetry to her life.

Turning from the scant biographical facts and what little can be surmised from them, we can glean from Brontë's writing valuable biographical information. First, *Wuthering Heights* provides a source to deduce Brontë's views on several topics: childhood, romantic love, death, alcoholism, and religion. It also shows her sense of humor, and that she was intellectually ahead of her time as a writer and a thinker. First, in the novel she shows that experiences from childhood define character and forge bonds like no other time in life: Nelly Dean, Heathcliff, and Hareton particularly demonstrate feelings for others solely because of childhood associations. From that we can deduce that her own childhood experiences, in particular the loss of her mother and her two sisters, had a notable impact on her personality, even though she was a very young child at the time of their deaths. Another trait we can deduce — she did not seem to be the sentimental type, as she depicts three instances of love as downright foolish: Edgar's for Catherine, Isabella's for Heathcliff, and Young Catherine's for Linton. Hindley's and Frances's deep affection for each other as newlyweds is also described as a bit silly. Even with its several nubile couples, the plot of the novel lacks a traditional love-story trajectory so popular with the Victorians. That absence of romance includes Heathcliff, often thought of as the epitome of a romantic lover. Heathcliff's attachment to Catherine is explicable given his unloved and outcast situation, but his love only achieves tragic and great romantic proportions once he is a mourner. Which brings me to another feature of her personality revealed by the novel: death must have occupied a large part of Brontë's thoughts. How could it not, given that in her novel she has twelve characters die and creates the greatest mourner in literary history, who is driven to unearth and embrace a corpse even after eighteen years. She explored in the novel, like no novelist had done before and perhaps none has done since, the topics of death and grief like (quite naturally) a poet. A third revealing element is her treatment of alcoholism. Alcoholism plays a notable role in *Wuthering Heights* as the cause of the downfall of Hindley Earnshaw. To assuage his grief, Hindley drinks, becomes addicted, and makes himself an easy prey for Heathcliff when he returns, leading to his complete ruin. From Brontë's creating this character, I deduce her understanding of the ravages of alcoholism and conclude that she placed it among the worst of afflictions. The dissipation of her brother, Branwell, would have given her a basis for that perspective. The omission of religious content in *Wuthering Heights* also reveals information about Brontë. Although Edgar Linton, we hear from Nelly Dean, has gone to church in an instance or two, religion plays no part in the characters' lives. The curate has learned to steer clear of the Heights, and no one turns to God and prayer when in need, such as when facing death, sorrow, or imprisonment, except Joseph. He, alone, makes religion part of his life and he is a zealot, self-serving in his beliefs, and hardly a laudable character. The irreligiousness is surprising for a Victorian woman and daughter of a clergyman; the lack of religious sentiment must lead one to suspect she had little traditional religious feeling herself. Related to the topic of religion is Lockwood's dream of the torturous sermon of Jabes Branderham. That episode affords us the opportunity of surmising another aspect of Brontë's personality. She must have had a sense of humor, contrary to the view one might have of a shy recluse. The sermon reflects a sharp satirical sense, eager to poke fun at sermonizing ministers. Other instances of humor arise as well. I have to imagine her chuckling to herself when she wrote the scene recounted in the letter of Isabella of her exasperating encounter with Joseph upon her arrival at Wuthering Heights in her newly acquired state of Mrs. Heathcliff. Likewise, when Joseph complains to Heathcliff about the loss of some shrubs and laments that he might actually have to think about "leaving the old place," Shakespearean comic relief comes to mind. Speaking of Joseph, we know also that Brontë had an uncanny ability to recreate the accents and speech of others and therefore had to be an acute observer and listener.

Last, the originality of her novel reveals that she was a fore-runner, from a literary and psychological perspective, and therefore possessed a self-sufficient way of thinking and a great intellect. She wrote a work that must owe its negative reception to the fact that it was not appropriate to its time and place in featuring domestic abuse, drunkenness, violence, an anti-hero as its central figure, a lack of didactic moral content and Christian virtue, and a frank and unflattering portrayal of romantic love. The fact that she included in her novel the realistic degradation and suffering of an alcoholic, also attests to her literary originality. From a psychological stand-point, Brontë recognized the life-long repercussions of childhood experiences a hundred years before Freud suggested the over-whelming impact of childhood. In her time, the idea predominated that breeding and lineage were the important factors in determining a person. Also current was the notion that a person's outlook and actions could be determined by following Christian precepts. She also presents with psychological perspi-cacity emotional co-dependence and the personal and variable nature of the grief process.

Brontë's poetry, like her novel, reveals a lot about her, as the pages ahead will tell. There is a partial caveat to the notion that her poetry expresses her own thoughts and feelings. Not every poetic sentiment can be strictly speaking attributed to Brontë as her own. She wrote poems from various perspectives and developed themes from several facets of a topic. That approach utilizes her "negative capability," a term that the poet John Keats originated to describe the ability of a poet to be outside himself and in the minds of other people or even creatures. Also, many of her poems have an underlying fictional world called Gondal that she and Anne invented as children and continued developing throughout their lives in conversations, in poetry, and perhaps also in prose stories. Therefore, proper names that appear in poems are Gondolian, and often the emotions expressed are attributed to a character. One can study Brontë's poems to parse together the Gondal narrative, which critics have done. For Gondal aficionados the interest in a certain poem hinges to some degree on its fit in the Gondal frame — who is speaking, to whom, and where. My hermeneutics do not afford Gondal much importance. First, knowing the whole story is not possible and any discernible story line is too fragmented to engage a reader as a narrative or to develop a character. I take the Gondal names just as I would any name that appears in a poem. As for the degree to which her own thoughts are voiced in Gondal poems, at times it seems that Brontë is writing dialogue for a character and others where she seems to be expressing her own mind or feelings. Even in a character's poetic dialogue, the poet, however negatively-capable, does not disappear; in a sense, we still hear her voice even when the words are spoken by a poetical character. Therefore the poems (whether or not Gondolian) give the following insights to Brontë's personality, which will be discussed in the chapters to follow. She loved nature and solitude; she thought almost obsessively about all aspects of death; she developed her own sense of spirituality, dispensing with conventional religion. She saw life as hardship and suffering and at times had a dire view of human nature, but she faced reality not without compensations: nature, associations formed in childhood and, most notably, the power of imagination, which could defeat even death.

CHAPTER TWO

Nature

The natural world made an appearance in poetry during the Romantic era, distinguishing Romantic poetry from that of the immediately preceding Neo-classical period. Nature, with its hills, lakes, streams, flowers, the ocean, the sun, the moon and stars appeared not only as a setting, but also as inspiration for and a topic of poetry. William Wordsworth, a quintessential Romantic poet, whose work spanned the years from 1789 to 1847, celebrated nature in his poems, finding inspiration in the mountainous Lake District of England. John Keats, who lived from 1795 to 1821, would also take his poetic canvas out of doors and depict in meter and rhyme all manner of birds and flowers, and would zero in like a telephoto lens on bees and gnats. His paean to nature, with the opening words "O Solitude!", celebrates the beauty, not of rugged mountains, but of the suburbs of London, which in his day were a bucolic escape from grime and noise. Also, a stubble field viewed on a Sunday walk inspired his poem "To Autumn."

It is impossible to know whether Brontë's inspiration to write poems about natural subjects came more from the Romantic poets or from her own life. There is no hard evidence about all the poets she read, but biographical information about the Brontës and the fact that the household was highly literate and poetical support the conclusion that she read the most notable Romantic poets: Robert Southey, Samuel Taylor Coleridge, George Gordon Lord Byron, William Wordsworth and John Keats. In that list, the big certainty is Byron and his influence, which I will mention from time to time in my discussions. She also read the Latin poets, and most assuredly William Shakespeare and John Milton, whose epic "Paradise Lost" was nearly memorized by her father.

Brontë's own reading aside, she hardly needed the suggestion that nature was an apt topic for poetry because she lived very much in the natural world. The image of Emily Brontë traversing and exploring the moors is one mythic element about her that is true. Today a visitor to the Brontë Parsonage can literally walk in the paths she trod and rest upon a boulder by a stream that she is reliably known to have frequented. From very young childhood, walking on the moors was a prime leisure activity for the Brontë sisters. Going for a walk of several miles over a deserted and rugged landscape originated with Mr. Brontë, who was a great walker. Walking was a prime method for her communing with nature; close to the ground and at the slow pace afforded by only two legs, walking gave her the opportunity to explore the flora and fauna that would be missed on horseback or carriage rides. Emily might have enjoyed a ride on horseback over the moors, however. In *Wuthering Heights*, she has the young Catherine galloping across the moors on her pony, Minnie. Horses were a large expense and beyond the means of Mr. Brontë, so walking served as the normal method of transportation. A walk of many miles was not a daunting proposition for the Brontës. Again *Wuthering Heights* provides illustrations: Mr. Earnshaw has walked forty miles from Liverpool at the beginning of the story, carrying the little child Heathcliff, and Lockwood and Nelly Dean think little of traversing the six miles to take them to Wuthering Heights and back to Thrushcross Grange.

In addition to loving her walks on the moors, Brontë appears from her poetry to have been passionate about the seasons, as they appear repeatedly and importantly in her poems. The impact of the change of seasons cannot be overlooked for any nineteenth-century inhabitant of the north of England, although her poetic sensibility no doubt enhanced her perception. Without electricity or heat, the arrival of winter could certainly be considered a grim event, hence the association in her poems of winter with death, sadness, and hardship. The month of June figures as a motif and is presented as glorious and golden, as it would have been after the bitter winter and wet spring of the north of England. Brontë also was particularly impressed by the wind, a common feature of life in Haworth. Wuthering Heights, as Lockwood tells us, is a name signifying the strong winds that race down the hillside and assault the house, causing the trees to slant one way "as if craving alms from the sun." In Brontë's poems the wind is a presence having various effects, from bringing back memories, to wielding a seductive power, to inducing spiritual experiences.

Emily Brontë for most of her life slept in a very small room that had been formed out of another room, and her bed was situated under a window with an unobstructed view of the sky. I can imagine that she made good use of it to observe the moon and stars, as she frequently depicts them and the effect they have to engender a feeling of another world beyond the mundane. Aside from leading to mystical experiences, the sky was a joy to her, if we can take her poetry as an indication. In a poem, "'Thou standest in the greenwood now,'" (which appears in the chapter "Love") a speaker in the poem reflects on the undeniably greater allure of the sun over the moon to express the greater attraction of one lover to another: "'I gazed upon the cloudless moon / And loved her all the night / Till morning came and radiant noon, / Then I forgot her light— // No, not forgot — eternally / Remains its memory dear; / But could the day seem dark to me / Because the night was fair?'" Yet, surprisingly, in another poem (appearing in this chapter) night is preferable to a sunny day. In depicting the moon, the sun, and nature generally, Brontë resists the poetic practice at the time of mythological allusion, the one exception being the phrase "Cynthia's silvery" light to describe the moon in one instance. That departure from tradition contributes not only to her poetry's originality and durability, but also its visual honesty. For example, Charlotte Brontë edited a poem of Emily's after her death to change the description of a willow's branches from "gleaming hair" to "dryad hair," a dryad being a mythological tree nymph. A small example, but it serves to show how Emily, free of a poetic convention of the time, was effective as a poet. She describes the tree as it looked in nature; Charlotte simply made an allusion. Indeed, if you see a willow tree in the sun, you can observe that the long weedy branches do look like hair and they do gleam.

Overall, nature plays a large and varied role in the poetry of Emily Brontë. Very often, a natural scene, complete with the description of a season, atmospheric conditions, and vegetation, comprises the opening stanzas solely as the setting, but nature *per se* does not center the poem thematically. Progressing from a natural setting to the development of an idea figures so frequently that the first few lines often give no indication of the topic of the poem. As with Shakespearean sonnets, the ultimate meaning of the poem appears at the end. In addition to making use of the natural world as a setting for a poem, Brontë uses nature as a point of comparison or contrast to the human condition. For example, the natural prospect and arrival of winter reflects mutability and presages human death. In other poems, the beauty of the natural world contrasts with a situation of sadness, which serves to deepen the pathos. Therefore, there are many poems that have a large element of nature that I have not included in this chapter because other thematic ideas predominate in them, and my process of classification is based on theme. Here, I have included poems in which Brontë presents nature itself as the topic for a thematic expression, particularly that nature has the power to console.

High waving heather, 'neath stormy blasts bending,
Midnight and moonlight and bright shining stars;
Darkness and glory rejoicingly blending,
Earth rising to heaven and heaven descending,
Man's spirit away from its drear dungeon sending,
Bursting the fetters and breaking the bars.

All down the mountain sides, wild forests lending
One mighty voice to the life-giving wind;
Rivers their banks in the jubilee rending,
Fast through the valleys a reckless course wending,
Wider and deeper their waters extending,
Leaving a desolate desert behind.

Shining and lowering and swelling and dying,
Changing for ever from midnight to noon;
Roaring like thunder, like soft music sighing,
Shadows on shadows advancing and flying,
Lightning-bright flashes the deep gloom defying,
Coming as swiftly and fading as soon.

"High waving heather" gives a sweeping and time-lapse view of nature to capture its contrasting and perpetually changing elements. The theme of this poem connects with the topic of spirituality because it depicts nature as an exhilarating and divine force that frees man's sprit from the bonds of life. Breaking chains is a hallmark motif in Brontë's poetry, as will be explored in the chapter "Captivity and Freedom," and typically signifies escape from the mundane world or even from life. Although I do not delve into her meter and rhyme, the feminine rhyme (the "ing" verb endings) bears mentioning here because its lively chanting rhythm conveys a sense of movement.

How still, how happy! Those are words
That once would scarce agree together;
I loved the plashing of the surge,
The changing heaven, the breezy weather,

More than smooth seas and cloudless skies
And solemn, soothing, softened airs
That in the forest woke no sighs
And from the green spray shook no tears.

How still, how happy! Now I feel
Where silence dwells is sweeter far
Than laughing mirth's most joyous swell
However pure its raptures are.

Come, sit down on this sunny stone:
'Tis wintry light o'er flowerless moors —

But sit — for we are all alone
And clear expand heaven's breathless shores.

I could think in the withered grass
Spring's budding wreaths we might discern;
The violet's eye might shyly flash
And young leaves shoot among the fern.

It is but thought — full many a night
The snow shall clothe those hills afar
And storms shall add a drearier blight
And winds shall wage a wilder war,

Before the lark may herald in
Fresh foliage twined with blossoms fair
And summer days again begin
Their glory-haloed crown to wear.

Yet my heart loves December's smile
As much as July's golden beam;
Then let us sit and watch the while
The blue ice curdling on the stream.

"How still, how happy" recounts an appreciation of quiet and
tranquility, even though such stillness lacks mirth and overt joy.
The first person speaker asks someone to sit with him or her and
contemplate the winter, mirthless yet peaceful like the state of
stillness described at the opening of the poem. Although Brontë
more often depicts winter as grim and sad, here that season is as
beautiful in its own way as a summer day.

The blue bell is the sweetest flower
That waves in summer air;
Its blossoms have the mightiest power
To soothe my spirit's care.

There is a spell in purple heath
Too wildly, sadly dear;
The violet has a fragrant breath
But fragrance will not cheer.

The trees are bare, the sun is cold,
And seldom, seldom seen;
The heavens have lost their zone of gold
The earth its robe of green;

And ice upon the balancing stream
Has cast its sombre shade
And distant hills and valleys seem
In frozen mist arrayed.

The blue bell cannot charm me now,
The heath has lost its bloom,
The violets in the glen below
They yield no sweet perfume.

But though I mourn the heather-bell
'Tis better far, away;
I know how fast my tears would swell
To see it smile to-day;

And that wood flower that hides so shy
Beneath its mossy stone
Its balmy scent and dewy eye:
'Tis not for them I moan.

It is the slight and stately stem,
The blossoms silvery blue,
The buds hid like a sapphire gem
In sheaths of emerald hue.

'Tis these that breathe upon my heart
A calm and softening spell
That if it makes the tear-drop start
Has power to soothe as well.

For these I weep, so long divided
Through winter's dreary day,
In longing weep — but most when guided
On withered banks to stray.

If chilly then the light should fall
Adown the dreary sky
And gild the dank and darkened wall
With transient brilliancy,

How do I yearn, how do I pine
For the time of flowers to come,
And turn me from the fading shine
To mourn the fields of home.

"The blue bell is the sweetest flower" laments the absence of flowers from a wintry landscape, most particularly the bluebell. The speaker so loves that flower that it provides a source of solace and its absence constitutes a great loss. The poem also expresses sadness at change, exemplified by the change of seasons, and thereby also suggests the topic of mutability.

How long will you remain? The midnight hour
Has tolled the last note from the minster tower.
Come, come: the fire is dead, the lamp burns low,
Your eyelids droop, a weight is on your brow.
Your cold hands hardly hold the useless pen;
Come: morn will give recovered strength again.

"No: let me linger; leave me, let me be
A little longer in this reverie.

I'm happy now, and would you tear away
My blissful dream, that never comes with day;
A vision dear, though false, for well my mind
Knows what a bitter waking waits behind?"

"Can there be pleasure in this shadowy room,
With windows yawning on intenser gloom,
And such a dreary wind so bleakly sweeping
Round walls where only you are vigil keeping?
Besides, your face has not a sign of joy,
And more than tearful sorrow fills your eye.
Look on those woods, look on that heaven lorn,
And think how changed they'll be to-morrow morn:
The dome of heaven expanding bright and blue,
The leaves, the green grass, sprinkled thick with dew,
And wet mists rising on the river's breast,
And wild birds bursting from their songless nest,
And your own children's merry voices chasing
The fancies grief, not pleasure, has been tracing."

"Aye, speak of these, but can you tell me why
Day breathes such beauty over earth and sky,
And waking sounds revive, restore again
The hearts that all night long have throbbed in pain?
Is it not that the sunshine and the wind
Lure from its self the mourner's woe-worn mind;
And all the joyous music breathing by
And all the splendour of that cloudless sky,
Re-give him shadowy gleams of infancy,
And draw his tired gaze from futurity?

"How long will you remain" expresses the idea that the beauty
of nature, in particular a summer morning, has a consoling power.
In this poem, two speakers converse; the first tries to console the
other, who is lost in a reverie that has given him or her some relief
from harsh reality, even though he or she appears mournful, sitting

in a dim and chilly room, at midnight. The first speaker reminds
the other that morning, in its beauty and brightness, cannot help
but bring happier thoughts and a renewed spirit. The second
speaker does not disagree with that conclusion, but points out that
the morning consoles for the same reason he or she has found some
solace by sitting in front of the dying fire at midnight: both are
times when one can get lost in thought and leave reality. The
reason nature raises the spirit is that it charms a person away from
thoughts of the future, with its grim reality, and lures one's
thoughts back to childhood. In lamenting the past, the poem also
expresses the sentiments of the poems included in the chapter
"Mutability." The quotation marks in the poem are confusing. The
first stanza represents words spoken by the first persona to the
other; nonetheless it does not appear in quotes. The second stanza
is the response of the second persona in the poem; the third is the
rejoinder of the first speaker, and the last, the conclusion of the
second persona. The word "lorn" means desolate or forsaken and
"infancy" means childhood, not the state of being an infant.

I've been wandering in the greenwoods,
And 'mid flowery, smiling plains;
I've been listening to the dark floods,
To the thrush's thrilling strains.

I have gathered the pale primrose,
And the purple violet sweet;
I've been where the asphodel grows,
And where lives the red deer fleet.

I've been to the distant mountain,
To the silver singing rill,
By the crystal murmuring fountain,
And the shady, verdant hill.

I've been where the poplar is springing
From the fair enamelled ground,

Where the nightingale is singing
With a solemn, plaintive sound.

"I've been wandering in the greenwoods" is a paean to nature:
its plains, waters, flowers, deer, and birds. Here, the speaker does
not relate his or her own emotions directly, but rather describes
what he or has seen, heard, or done while visiting flowery plains
and far away mountains. The poem ends on a wistful note with the
song of the nightingale. That bird must be a very vocal one. Brontë
has apparently heard it singing, and John Keats, inspired by its
song, wrote one of his greatest works, "Ode to a Nightingale." The
thrush also has spoken to both poets, judging from the fourth line
of this poem and Keats's poem entitled "What the Thrush Said."

Shall Earth no more inspire thee,
Thou lonely dreamer now?
Since passion may not fire thee
Shall Nature cease to bow?

Thy mind is ever moving
In regions dark to thee;
Recall its useless roving —
Come back and dwell with me.

I know my mountain breezes
Enchant and soothe thee still —
I know my sunshine pleases
Despite thy wayward will.

When day with evening blending
Sinks from the summer sky,
I've seen thy spirit bending
In fond idolatry.

I've watched thee every hour;
I know my mighty sway,

I know my magic power
To drive thy griefs away.

Few hearts to mortals given
On earth so wildly pine;
Yet none would ask a Heaven
More like this Earth than thine.

Then let my winds caress thee;
Thy comrade let me be —
Since nought beside can bless thee,
Return and dwell with me.

"Shall Earth no more inspire thee" again personifies nature, overall in this case, rather than one particular aspect. Frequently the wind is personified, as will be discussed in the chapter "Imagination." Personification is not limited to nature in Brontë's poetry. For example, she also personifies Death and, as such, Death delivers the admonitory monologue contained in another poem, "I'll come when thou art saddest." Another good example is her personification of Hope, in "Hope was but a timid friend." Personification is in the tradition of the allegorical work *The Pilgrim's Progress* by John Bunyan which Brontë most certainly knew. In the poem, "Nature" addresses someone, "a lonely dreamer," whose voice is not heard. Nature has returned like an old acquaintance to remind him or her that Nature can assuage her ennui, grief, and pining. In the penultimate stanza, Nature sums up the lonely dreamer's outlook by saying that few mortals suffer as much as he or she has done, yet would not wish for heaven to be anything other than like this earth. I find those lines supportive of my view that Brontë to a large extent found mortal existence sorrowful and inadequate, but was consoled by nature. This poem also expresses an idea that appears in *Wuthering Heights*, that heaven is a personal extension of one's desire and not an objective state described by scripture or ministers. Heathcliff's heaven is nothing more than dying to join Catherine in the grave.

Nelly Dean seems to accept that an objective heaven exists, but
wonders if certain idiosyncratic individuals like Heathcliff could
be happy there.

> **Ah! Why, because the dazzling sun**
> Restored my earth to joy
> Have you departed, every one,
> And left a desert sky?
>
> All through the night, your glorious eyes
> Were gazing down in mine,
> And with a full heart's thankful sighs
> I blessed that watch divine!
>
> I was at peace, and drank your beams
> As they were life to me
> And revelled in my changeful dreams
> Like petrel on the sea.
>
> Thought followed thought — star followed star
> Through boundless regions on,
> While one sweet influence, near and far,
> Thrilled through and proved us one.
>
> Why did the morning rise to break
> So great, so pure a spell,
> And scorch with fire the tranquil cheek
> Where your cool radiance fell?
>
> Blood-red he rose, and arrow-straight
> His fierce beams struck my brow:
> The soul of Nature sprang elate
> But mine sank sad and low!
>
> My lids closed down — yet through their veil
> I saw him blazing still;

And bathe in gold the misty dale,
And flash upon the hill.

I turned me to the pillow then
To call back Night, and see
Your worlds of solemn light, again
Throb with my heart and me!

It would not do — the pillow glowed
And glowed both roof and floor,
And birds sang loudly in the wood
And fresh winds shook the door.

The curtains waved, the wakened flies
Were murmuring round my room.
Imprisoned there, till I should rise
And give them leave to roam.

O Stars and Dreams and Gentle Night;
O Night and Stars return!
And hide me from the hostile light
That does not warm, but burn —

That drains the blood of suffering men;
Drinks tears, instead of dew:
Let me sleep through his blinding reign,
And only wake with you!

"Ah! Why, because the dazzling sun" laments the rising of the
sun that replaces the stars, with which the speaker has had a
peaceful, spiritual, and joyful communion during the night.
"Petrel," in the third stanza, are sea birds that fly close to the
ocean's surface. This poem is unusual for Brontë in associating the
sun with excess and suffering. Vampire-like, the speaker finds the
daylight harsh and destructive, even though the "dazzling sun"
brings joy to the earth. Taking this poem literally, the speaker

describes a mystical and consuming experience brought on simply by gazing at the stars; she achieves a state of unity with nature and a spiritual sensation of "one sweet influence." In that regard this poem resembles those in the chapter "Spirituality." A more material interpretation would suggest that the speaker has a heightened perception of nature and relishes the quiet and beauty of the night for star-gazing. Such a state of mind would be reminiscent of Lockwood's description to Nelly Dean of how people who have few distractions in life and live in a solitary way develop faculties of observation and an interest in things that would seem normal or hardly noticeable to others. He says of such people, addressing Nelly Dean: "You have been compelled to cultivate your reflective faculties, for want of occasions for frittering your life away in silly trifles." Relating that thought to the modern world, it would seem that people who are bombarded by images on a screen would have little attention to direct to the stars outside the window; and in brightly lit cities, they might not even be able to see the stars. Nonetheless, it does take special powers of the mind to be so transported by an element of the natural world. On a metaphorical level, the poem means that a meditative and inner existence is preferable to action and the rigors of life. One can also conclude that, metaphorically, night represents death, which is preferable to day, which means a return to earth and human existence. The array of interpretations aside, the third stanza from the end arrests my attention because of its careful focus on the insect world. It reminds me of Keats's "wailful choir" of gnats in "To Autumn." It also grounds the poem in the reality of Brontë's own bedroom; at the parsonage she would shoo the flies out of the door rather than swat them.

> **Often rebuked, yet always back returning**
> To those first feeling that were born with me,
> And leaving busy chase of wealth and learning
> For idle dreams of things which cannot be:

To-day, I will seek not the shadowy region;
Its unsustaining vastness waxes drear;
And visions rising, legion after legion,
Bring the unreal world too strangely near.

I'll walk, but not in old heroic traces,
And not in paths of high morality,
And not among the half-distinguished faces,
The clouded forms of long-past history.

I'll walk where my own nature would be leading:
It vexes me to choose another guide:
Where the gray flocks in ferny glens are feeding;
Where the wild wind blows on the mountain side.

What have those lonely mountains worth revealing?
More glory and more grief than I can tell:
The earth that wakes one human heart to feeling
Can centre both the worlds of Heaven and Hell.

"Often rebuked, yet always back returning" might be Emily's poem or it might have been written by Charlotte describing Emily, in her efforts to create an understanding of her deceased sister. The second stanza's rejection of the "unreal world" is at odds with every other poetic statement Emily made on that topic and therefore sounds more like Charlotte's words. I have included it because the statement of nature is consistent with Emily's expressions on the topic: the mountains can tell all that man need know — sufficient to reconcile heaven and hell. Rather than, as Keats stated, "beauty is truth, truth beauty," this poem posits that "nature is truth and truth nature" — a very similar statement really, since the beauty to which Keats was referring included nature.

CHAPTER THREE

Mutability

Mutability connotes the changes, like them or not, brought by the implacable course of existence. One cannot use the word, at least when discussing poetry, without thinking of the poem of Percy Bysshe Shelley, "Mutability," that defines the word so well:

> We are as clouds that veil the midnight moon;
>   How restlessly they speed, and gleam, and quiver,
> Streaking the darkness radiantly! — yet soon
>   Night closes round, and they are lost for ever:
>
> Or like forgotten lyres, whose dissonant strings
>   Give various response to each varying blast,
> To whose frail frame no second motion brings
>   One mood of modulation like the last.
>
> We rest. — A dream has power to poison sleep;
>   We rise. — One wandering thought pollutes the day;
> We feel, conceive or reason, laugh or weep;
>   Embrace fond woe, or cast our cares away:
>
> It is the same! — For, be it joy or sorrow,
>   The path of its departure still is free:
> Man's yesterday may ne'er be like his morrow;
>   Nought may endure but Mutability.

After reading Brontë's poems, one might see similarities to Shelley's poem not only in theme but motif; however, that comparative essay is beyond my present purpose. Poems addressing mutability fall under the literary term "elegy" and have a long and constant history, from Greek and Roman works, through the poetry of today. Elegies have also come to include more particularly a sustained lament in verse upon the loss of a certain person. As for the second and narrower use of the word "elegy," Brontë did not write such poems to any one of the several family members and close acquaintances whose deaths she experienced. When she does mention the death of a particular individual, he or she frequently seems to be a Gondal character, such that we could coin a term for those poems, calling them fictional elegy. Gondal or not, her poems dealing primarily with the death of someone, in which the topic of death predominates, will appear under the chapter "Death." Brontë wrote a number of poems that deal thematically with mutability and that can be termed elegies in the first and broader sense. Love lost, childhood over, dreams abandoned, old acquaintances gone appear in these poems. Brontë creates the mood of nostalgia that accompanies mutability through settings of autumn and mists and through diction, using words that look back in time, such as "long-forgotten," "earlier days," and "old feelings." There is on the whole little consolation for the sadness brought by change, and the various poetic personae must suffer the tyranny of happy memories. Even when the speaker in a poem is able to revive the past in his or her thoughts, it at best appears like a dream.

Music and musical instruments play a part in these poems, quite appropriately given the ability of a song to take a person back to another time and place. Music will also come up saliently in the poems in the chapter "Spirituality" because music forms part of the mystical experiences described in those poems. Emily would have included music in her poems because she was musical. There was a piano at the parsonage, and Emily was the most musical member of the household. When she went to Brussels at the age of twenty-three, staying there eight months to learn French, she had the opportunity to further her study of the piano and became an accomplished pianist. The upright piano was in Mr. Brontë's study. As a visitor to the Brontë Parsonage, you can stand at the threshold of his study, see the piano still tucked against the left wall, and imagine how the loud and soft tones must have resounded and floated through a house that had stone floors and no curtains or carpets.

Harp of wild and dream-like strain,
When I touch thy strings,
Why dost thou repeat again
Long-forgotten things?

Harp, in other, earlier days,
I could sing to thee;
And not one of all my lays
Vexed my memory.

But now, if I awake a note
That gave me joy before,
Sounds of sorrow from thee float,
Changing evermore.

Yet, still steeped in memory's dyes,
They come sailing on,
Darkening all my summer skies,
Shutting out my sun.

"Harp of wild and dream-like strain" laments mutability in two ways. The speaker of the poem yearns for that time in the past when she could play the harp without feeling sad; now its tones sound wild and like a dream. She also ponders the "long-forgotten things" of which the absence produces a sorrow that darkens the summer sky. Memories provoked by the music are the dark culprit that steals her joy. To me, this poem, with the harp and the word "lays" for songs, evokes a medieval or Pre-Raphaelite image.

For him who struck thy foreign string,
I ween this heart hath ceased to care;
Then why dost thou such feelings bring
To my sad spirit, old guitar?

It is as if the warm sunlight
In some deep glen should lingering stay,
When clouds of tempest and of night
Had wrapt the parent orb away.

It is as if the glassy brook
Should image still its willows fair,
Though years ago the woodman's stroke
Laid low in dust their gleaming hair.

Even so, guitar, thy magic tone
Has moved the tear and waked the sigh,
Has bid the ancient torrent flow
Although its very source is dry!

"For him who struck thy foreign string" is a monologue in which a female voice questions how she can still feel sadness at the memory of "him" when she thought she was long beyond caring. It is a Gondal poem, and the speaker is Augusta Geraldine Almeda, as indicated by the initials A.G.A. at the top of the poem. Beyond telling us that the speaker is a woman, the identity of the speaker means little or nothing to one's appreciation of the poem and its plaintive, nostalgic imagery. As in the previous poem, music is the catalyst to provoke thoughts of the past. An unnamed man played the guitar. Now, years after she ended her relationship with him, she herself has strummed the guitar or heard someone else playing it, and "its magic tone," associated with him, revives his memory. The use of the word "ween" in the first stanza is an archaism — the word means "think" and was not used in current speech even in Brontë's time. The image in the last stanza of a source that has run dry echoes the absence of emotion, the heart that had ceased to care, described in the first stanza. This poem contains two beautiful and apt images to capture the feeling, which we must all have had, that things should still be as they once were. In the first, "the parent orb" (the sun) should still be lighting up the glen even when obscured by clouds. In the second, the willow tree that used to border a stream, even after many years of absence, should still be reflected in the glassy waters.

How few, of all the hearts that loved,
Are grieving for thee now!
And why should mine, to-night, be moved
With such a sense of woe?

Too often, thus, when left alone
Where none my thoughts can see,
Comes back a word, a passing tone
From thy strange history.

Sometimes I seem to see thee rise,
A glorious child again —
All virtues beaming from thine yes
That ever honoured men —

Courage and Truth, a generous breast
Where Love and Gladness lay;
A being whose very Memory blest
And made the mourner gay.

O fairly spread thy early sail
And fresh and pure and free
Was the first impulse of the gale
That urged life's wave for thee!

Why did the pilot, too confiding,
Dream o'er that Ocean's foam
And trust in Pleasure's careless guiding
To bring his vessel home?

For well he knew what dangers frowned,
What mists would gather dim;
What rocks and shelves and sands lay round
Between the port and him.

The very brightness of the sun,
The splendor of the main,
The wind that bore him wildly on
Should not have warned in vain.

An anxious gazer from the shore,
I marked the whitening wave,
And wept above thy fate the more
Because I could not save.

It recks not now, when all is over;
But yet my heart will be
A mourner still, though friend and lover
Have both forgotten thee!

"How few, of all the hearts that loved" has as a title "E.W. to
A.G.A." which designates the speaker and his or her listener.
However, at first the speaker rhetorically addresses the departed,
a man, and then from the sixth stanza, he or she refers to the
deceased at times in the third person. Turning to the sense of muta-
bility in this poem, this time, not music, but a word or tone similar
to that of the deceased resurrects him and his history. This poem
figures in the category of mutability rather than love or death
because the speaker was never enamored of the deceased; she or he
knew him well from his childhood, but refers to others who were
his friends or lovers.

Also, it is not the death or ensuing grief that troubles the
speaker — he or she has not thought about the deceased for some
time. Rather, true to the nostalgia inherent in the idea of muta-
bility, the mind has wandered to former times from a hint of the
past. Such sadness produced by the lure of the past, rather than by

the strength of current or recent bonds, affects Nelly Dean in *Wuthering Heights* upon hearing the news of Hindley's death: "Ancient associations lingered round my heart; I sat down in the porch, and wept as for a blood relation . . ." The poem contains an extended metaphor comparing sailing on the sea to living. The world's storm troubled sea, an image for life, is a frequent trope in Brontë's poetry, and here Brontë continues the metaphor to include the port or shore for death. The word "recks" in the first line of the final stanza is an archaic way of saying "something is of no importance." What a useful and memorable line, "It recks not now, when all is over."

Where were ye all? And where wert thou?
I saw an eye that shone like thine;
But dark curls waved around his brow,
And his stern glance was strange to mine.

And yet a dreamlike comfort came
Into my heart and anxious eye;
And, trembling yet to hear his name,
I bent to listen watchfully.

His voice, though never heard before,
Still spoke to me of years gone by;
It seemed a vision to restore
That brought the hot tears to my eye.

"Where were ye all? And where wert thou?" depicts how memories of a long lost person arise upon meeting someone who bears some similar trait, in this case, similar eyes. The speaker's anxious words convey the eagerness, the momentary comfort, and the fast following sadness upon seeing some similarity to a person who is gone forever. As in many of the poems that contemplate the past, remembrance has a dreamlike quality. This poem is identifiable as a Gondal poem by the letters A.G.A, which appear under the date; they are the initials of a Gondal character that is a mainstay of the saga, Augusta Geraldine Almeda. As noted before, that fact has little if any relevance to one's reading of the poem.

Mild the mist upon the hill,
Telling not of storms to-morrow;
No; the day has wept its fill,
Spent its store of silent sorrow.

Oh, I'm gone back to the days of youth,
I am a child once more;
And 'neath my father's sheltering roof,
And near the old hall door,

I watch the cloudy evening fall,
After a day of rain:
Blue mists, sweet mists of summer pall
The horizon's mountain-chain.

The damp stands in the long, green grass
As thick as morning's tears;
And dreamy scents of fragrance pass
That breathe of other years.

"Mild the mist upon the hill" presents a common strain in Brontë's poetry, that the changes since childhood are not happy ones. Sorrow plagues the speaker of the poem, but he or she is transported back to the happier time of childhood by a misty damp evening, such as those from that time in the past. Nature further invokes memories with its summer scents that recall those of former years. So, music, a word or tone of voice, a similar pair of eyes, and here a misty day can all conjure the past. Again, the motif of dreams appears. As in the immediately preceding poem, thoughts of the past are described as having a dream-like quality; here the scent in the air is "dreamy." Similarly, in the first of these poems, the harp produces "dreamlike strains," and the past is also a dream in the immediately following poem. One also encounters a variation of the notion that the past is like a dream in a poem placed in the chapter "Love," in which, looking ahead rather than back, the speaker projects, in some of my favorite Brontë lines, that she will become like a dream to her former lover: "Day by day some dreary token / Will forsake thy memory / Till at last all old links broken / I shall be a dream to thee."

It is too late to call thee now:
I will not nurse that dream again;
For every joy that lit my brow
Would bring its after-storm of pain.

Besides, the mist is half withdrawn;
The barren mountain-side lies bare;
And sunshine and awaking morn
Paint no more golden visions there.

Yet, ever in my grateful breast,
Thy darling shade shall cherished be;
For God alone doth know how blest
My early years have been in thee!

"It is too late to call thee now" differs in its expression of mutability from her more usual view in that there is a clear consolation at the end for the pain brought by change and loss: childhood and knowing how fortunate he or she was to have shared those early years with the person who is now gone. However, before the poem takes that reconciliatory tone, the speaker decries remembrance because of the overwhelming pain that follows. In the second stanza, Brontë depicts mutability with the image of a bare mountain on which the morning sunshine no longer glows.

The wind, I hear it sighing
With Autumn's saddest sound;
Withered leaves as thick are lying
As spring-flowers on the ground.

This dark night has won me
To wander far away;
Old feelings gather fast upon me
Like vultures round their prey.

Kind were they once, and cherished,
But cold and cheerless now;
I would their lingering shades had perished
When their light left my brow.

'Tis like old age pretending
The softness of a child,
My altered, hardened spirit bending
To meet their fancies wild.

Yet could I with past pleasures
Past woe's oblivion buy,
That by the death of my dearest treasures
My deadliest pains might die,

O then another daybreak
Might haply dawn above,
Another summer gild my cheek,
My soul, another love.

"The wind, I hear it sighing" begins by creating a somber feeling: the season is autumn, the leaves are withered, and even the wind makes a wistful sound. Sometimes wandering off in thought brings an escape, or at least a dream-like state, but not in his poem. The thoughts of the past descend like vultures. To capture the idea of irrevocability, Brontë compares retrieving the past to the inability of an aged person to appear childlike again. The only way to love again or feel happiness is by annihilating memories. Like the previous poem, any relief derived from memories cannot outweigh the concomitant pain: in the penultimate stanza of this poem, the speaker declares that he or she would be willing to give up cherished memories to eliminate the pain caused by the loss, in this case the loss of a beloved person. That sentiment stands quite contrary to the famous lines written years later by Alfred Lord Tennyson in *In Memoriam*: "I hold it true, what'er befall; / I feel it, when I sorrow most; / 'Tis better to have loved and lost / Than never to have loved at all."

CHAPTER FOUR

Love

Poetry can express themes on diverse topics, but one of the most fundamental subjects for poetry is love, particularly declarations of passion and descriptions of its attendant feelings. Thus, that topical native to the poetic habitat has flourished in poetry from the ancient world to the Victorian era and in diverse cultures. Emily Brontë wrote a few poems in the typical tradition of relating the throes of passionate love. Her poem "At such a time, in such a spot" most notably hits the target with this stanza that closes the poem: "Oh could it forever be that I might so adore, / I'd ask for all eternity to make a paradise for me, / my love and nothing more." However, Brontë did not stop with passionate declarations, understanding that a relationship runs its course — it waxes or wans, but eventually ends one way or the other. Lovers in her poems are unrequited, constant, faithless, slighted, or won by new lovers who supersede the old. Treating the topic of love in non-ideal and ending stages is far less typical to poetic literature. Brontë wrote several "break-up poems," but I can think of only one other in the literary canon, a poem by Charles Algernon Swinburne, entitled "Before Parting." I highly recommend it. As part of her comprehensive treatment of the topic of romantic love, she recognizes not only the parting of lovers through a break-up, but also the untimely end by death. In some instances a poem depicts how death, even though it severs the relationship, creates an even greater appreciation of, or attachment to, the deceased; in others, death is the first step in loosening the bonds of affection. The former effect figures as the more typical construct when considering Emily Brontë because the lover who suffers an enduring attachment to the departed appears in *Wuthering Heights* in the characters of Hindley, Edgar, and most notably Heathcliff. Hindley cannot recover from the death of his wife Francis and gives himself to "reckless dissipation." Edgar and Heathcliff persevere in their attachment to Catherine until their own deaths. Edgar has some consolation in his daughter, Catherine, whereas Heathcliff, who has never cared for anyone else, is the most bereft and therefore the greatest mourner. There are two poems recognizable as channeling Edgar and Heathcliff as loving mourners, "Cold in the Earth" and "If grief for grief can touch thee," respectively. Heathcliff stands out as extreme in his posthumous passion, driven to unearth Catherine's corpse years after her death. Although there is a lover or two in Brontë's poems who languish at a loved one's grave, no other goes as far as Heathcliff — indeed his action hardly has a literary equal. The only other instance to rival that grave scene occurs in John Keats's poem "Isabella," in which the eponymous character digs up the corpse of her lover and brings home his head for safekeeping in a pot under a basil plant.

Despite Heathcliff's monomania for Catherine after her death, I strongly urge caution in seeing his relationship with Catherine as a great romance, by remembering just how asexual their relationship is. Heathcliff and Catherine are virtually brother and sister. (Incidentally, although there is no way to know if Brontë got the idea of a quasi-incestuous match from the example of Byron and his half-sister, Augusta, it is possible that she did. She knew about Byron's life and was certainly influenced by his poetry in her writing.) Further, when Catherine raises the prospect of marrying Heathcliff in her conversation in the kitchen with Nelly Dean, she reveals her ignorance about marriage in suggesting that by marrying Edgar she will be able to establish a friendly ménage à trois that includes Heathcliff. Catherine lives happily with Edgar until Heathcliff shows up after several years, and Heathcliff, although bent on creating trouble, does not think that Catherine will divorce Edgar or run away with him. They mostly quarrel like petulant children, and Heathcliff takes up a flirtation and marries Isabella Linton under Catherine's nose, although admittedly he does that to get revenge on Linton. Heathcliff does make declarations to Nelly Dean about his selfless devotion to Catherine when she falls ill, and he and Catherine finally act like lovers during their last meeting in her bedroom once it is clear that Catherine is dying. In both those scenes and throughout the history of those two characters in the novel, it is clear that their attachment has been forged by the bonds of childhood, and Heathcliff is the more bound of the two because he is entirely dependent upon Catherine for his happiness and associates her with himself because he has never had anyone else of importance in his life. Is such a state of dependence romantic love? Once Catherine dies, his enormous grief adopts the manners of passionate love. Other depictions of love in *Wuthering Heights* underscore the fatuity of passion: Edgar and Isabella are both smitten and wind up with mates far different than imagined through the lens of love. I conclude, then, that it is less in her novel and more in her poetry that a reader finds a traditional and affirmative expression of passionate love.

The Gondal saga sets the stage for most of Brontë's love poems, whether depicting passion, constancy, faithlessness, or the end of an erstwhile attachment. There are, as a result, a number of Gondal names in these poems. Even if one considered it important to know who these characters are in the Gondal story line, it would not be possible; happily, their identity is not necessary to value the poem, as the names can be taken like any other name mentioned in a poem. As discussed in the biographical section above, Emily and her sister Anne created as children an imaginary land of Gondal and peopled it with numerous characters. Like a current made-for-television saga, Gondal is a world of battles, treachery, prisons, and loves won and lost. Emily and Anne continued to invent episodes throughout their lives even into adulthood. In fact, the world of Gondal seemed more important to Emily than the real world. When she uncharacteristically left home for a trip with Anne to York, her only written comments about the outing stated that they had added to the Gondal story while away. Also, when she wrote one of her few extant notes in which she reflected what the future might bring to her and her sisters, she wondered what would be happening with the

Gondolians in the future. I think that Brontë's main interest in writing love poems was to record a Gondal plot development. In short, that imaginary world served as the inspiration rather than her own life and her own experiences because Brontë's love life, so to speak, was nonexistent. Charlotte, by contrast, developed a painful crush on Monsieur Heger, her teacher in Brussels, and eventually married the Reverend Arthur Bell Nicholls, one of her father's curates, although less out of infatuation, than being won over by his persistence and the realization that there were no other suitors. Not to say that she was not happily married; it appears that she was. One available bachelor, while the Brontë sisters were at the age for romance, was their father's curate at the time, William Weightman. Anne and Charlotte probably both found him of interest, but he seemed to be playing the field and was only flirting at the Brontë household. Emily seemed to have remained unaffected. Perhaps her "negative capability," or simply her imagination, underlies expressions of romantic love in her poems. Some fans of Emily Brontë have been desperate to find a love interest for her. I have never felt that she needed one to write what she wrote, nor is there any factual evidence of one.

The discussion about writing from experience raises a fundamental art / life question: can one depict something not actually lived or felt? There are those who believe that Brontë must have had some clandestine lover or else she could not have written about love. I would respond that she wrote about battles and dungeons and had never experienced either of those. Her "experience" was formed from what she read, observed, and imagined. Her lack of personal involvement stands in contrast to the love sonneteers who had their own experiences to fuel their poems. The more the wonder that Brontë succeeded in capturing the gamut of romantic love's vicissitudes and raptures. John Keats wrote in a letter, describing the difference between his process and that of Byron: "You speak of Lord Byron and me. There is this great difference between us: he describes what he sees — I describe what I imagine. Mine is the hardest task . . ." Indeed, as was hers.

Now trust a heart that trusts in you,
And firmly say the word "Adieu";
Be sure, wherever I may roam,
My heart is with your heart at home;

Unless there be no truth on earth,
And vows meant true are nothing worth,
And mortal man have no control
Over his own unhappy soul;

Unless I change in every thought,
And memory will restore me nought,
And all I have of virtue die
Beneath far Gondal's Foreign sky.

The mountain peasant loves the heath
Better than richest plains beneath;
He would not give one moorland wild
For all the fields that ever smiled;

And whiter brows than yours may be,
And rosier cheeks my eyes may see,
And lightening looks from orbs divine
About my pathway burn and shine;

But that pure light, changeless and strong,
Cherished and watched and nursed so long;
That love that first its glory gave
Shall be my pole star to the grave.

"Now trust a heart that trusts in you" depicts a faithful, more than passionate, lover who is going away for some unstated reason. It is a Gondal poem, so the speaker, who by inference is male, most likely is off on a voyage, a mission, or to engage in a battle. Addressing his farewell to his lover directly, the speaker declares that if there is any truth on earth, his vows of devotion are true.

He acknowledges that others might be more beautiful than she is, but he compares her to the heath, which he finds dearer than tame and pleasant fields. One reason for the strong attachment is that the lover has been long cherished and was his first love, presumably known at a young age. A recurring idea in her poetry and in *Wuthering Heights* is the importance of childhood: it is the crucial time for determining a person's character, constitutes the only really happy time of life, and sets the stage for forming enduring bonds of affection, as in this poem.

Geraldine, the moon is shining
With so soft, so bright a ray;
Seems it not that eve, declining,
Ushered in a fairer day?

While the wind is whispering only,
Far — across the water borne,
Let us in this silence lonely
Sit beneath the ancient thorn.

Wild the road, and rough and dreary;
Barren all the moorland round;
Rude the couch that rests us weary;
Mossy stone and heathy ground.

But, when winter storms were meeting
In the moonless, midnight dome,
Did we heed the tempest's beating,
Howling round our spirits' home?

No; that tree with branches riven,
Whitening in the whirl of snow,
As it tossed against the heaven,
Sheltered happy hearts below —

And at Autumn's mild returning
Shall our feet forget the way?
And in Cynthia's silver morning,
Geraldine, wilt thou delay?

"Geraldine, the moon is shining" has a title, "Song by Julius Brenzaida to G.S." identifying it not only as a Gondal poem, but a "song" written by a Gondal character. The two lovers, or maybe erstwhile lovers, are traveling across the moors, and though the landscape is harsh and they are weary, the moon is bright and the weather mild. The speaker attempts to revive Geraldine's interest by reminding her how they were once happy together out on the moors despite a raging storm. Now that the night is inviting, will she not return to that spot, or metaphorically return to her former feelings for the speaker. The notion of being happy on the moors even in dreadful weather brings to mind Heathcliff's and Catherine's happy escapades on the moors as children. The phrase "Cynthia's silver morning" is an allusion to the Greek goddess of the moon. The mythological allusion is unusual for Brontë; maybe she allowed it on this occasion for its alliteration with the word "silver," or maybe she decided that the fictional author of the song, Julius Brenzaida, would have been partial to that allusion. The following poem is the sequel to this one.

I knew not 'twas so dire a crime
To say the word, Adieu;
But this shall be the only time
My slighted heart shall sue.

The wild moorside, the winter morn,
The gnarled and ancient tree —
If in your breast they waken scorn,
Shall wake the same in me.

I can forget black eyes and brows,
And lips of rosy charm,

If you forget the sacred vows
Those faithless lips could form.

If hard commands can tame your love,
Or prison walls can hold,
I would not wish to grieve above
A thing so false and cold.

And there are bosoms bound to mine
With links both tried and strong;
And there are yes whose lightning shine
Has warmed and blessed me long:

Those eyes shall make my only day,
Shall set my spirit free,
And chase the foolish thoughts away
That mourn your memory!

"I knew not 'twas so dire a crime," of the same title as the pre-
ceding poem, answers the question about Geraldine's affections
— she in fact does not share the speaker's feelings for their for-
mer times together and even scorns the scene of their past
romance.

Spurned and angry, the speaker indulges in some name calling
then declares he has another lover who will help him get over her.
In this break-up poem the slighted lover is determined not to
pine.

At such a time, in such a spot,
The world seems made of light;
Our blissful hearts remember not
How surely follows night.

I cannot, Alfred, dream of aught
That casts a shade of woe;
That heaven is reigning in my thought,

Which wood and wave and earth have caught
From skies that overflow.

That heaven which my sweet lover's brow
Has won me to adore,
Which from his blue eyes beaming now
Reflects a still intenser glow
Than nature's heaven can pour.

I know our souls are all divine;
I know that when we die,
What seems the vilest, even like thine
A part of God himself shall shine
In perfect purity.

But coldly breaks November's day;
It changes, charmless all;
Unmarked, unloved, they pass away;
We do not wish one hour to stay,
Nor sigh at evening's fall.

And glorious is the gladsome rise
Of June's rejoicing morn;
And who with unregretful eyes
Can watch the lustre leave its skies
To twilight's shade forlorn?

Then art thou not my golden June
All mist and tempest free?
As shines earth's sun in summer noon
So heaven's sun shines in thee.

Let others seek its beams divine
In cell and cloister drear;
But I have found a fairer shrine
And happier worship here.

By dismal rites they win their bliss —
By penance, fasts, and fears;
I have one rite: a gentle kiss;
One penance: tender tears.

O could it thus forever be
That I might so adore;
I'd ask for all eternity
To make a paradise for me,
My love — and nothing more!

"At such a time, in such a spot" does not have a title so much as a designation of the characters involved: "A.G.A. to A.S." This poem reigns as Brontë's purest expression of requited passionate love and as an exemplary love poem, particularly considering the opening stanza and the last four stanzas. Those last four stanzas build a metaphor that equates love to religious worship to the apotheosis of paradise in the last stanza. The setting is not defined, but it appears to be November, even though the besotted speaker is oblivious to the autumnal time of year, feeling only that the world is made of light in the presence of her lover. Despite the season, he (her love) is June, with an even brighter glow than the June sun, having a celestial radiance, as if he is divine. His stature as a god fits the comparison of love to religion, mentioned above.

The speaker justifies her sentiment that he is divine by professing her belief that their souls are divine. One part of the poem puzzles me, and I wonder if the ideas expressed there pertain to some other incident in the Gondal story. Why does she refer to something vile about Alfred, with the lines in the fourth stanza, "What seems the vilest, even like thine . . ." I also wonder about the change to referring to Alfred in the third person in the third stanza. It is notable that the speaker's ebullience falters only once, at the very beginning with the wistful admission that, "Our blissful hearts remember not / How surely follows night."

If grief for grief can touch thee,
If answering woe for woe,
If any ruth can melt thee,
Come to me now!

I cannot be more lonely,
More drear I cannot be!
My worn heart throbs so wildly
'Twill break for thee.

And when the world despises,
When heaven repels my prayer,
Will not mine angel comfort?
Mine idol hear?

Yes, by the tears I've poured
By all my hours of pain,
O I shall surely win thee,
Beloved, again!

"If grief for grief can touch thee" lends itself to two interpreta-
tions. One proposes that the speaker is an anguished, spurned lover
who expresses his determination to reunite with his beloved. His
desperate and heartbroken plea seems doomed to fail, since woe,
loneliness and pain, however profound, have no power to bring
about a desired outcome. He addresses her, but his words sound
rhetorical, as one senses that she is not present — which leads to
the second interpretation. She is absent because she is dead, and
the words are those of a bereft lover who will only regain his
beloved through death. In that light, the poem presages
Heathcliff, who resembles the speaker of this poem, when he
throws open the window after Lockwood's dream and cries out for
Catherine to come to him or when he calls out to Catherine to take
pity and haunt him. The emotion and diction in the third stanza
also appear in *Wuthering Heights* to describe his situation: Catherine

is his idol and angel, the world despises him, and heaven has rejected him, as he has rejected heaven.

The word "ruth" used in the first stanza means pity or compassion, and might be thought archaic even for Brontë; however, in a letter that Charlotte wrote describing Emily's behavior during her final illness, she uses that word: "Day by day, when I saw with what a front she met suffering, I looked on her with an anguish of wonder and love. I have seen nothing like it; but indeed I have never seen her parallel in anything. Stronger than a man, simpler than a child her nature stood alone. The awful point was that, while full of ruth for others, on herself she had no pity; the spirit was inexorable to the flesh; from the trembling hands, the unnerved limbs, the fading eyes, the same service was exacted as they had rendered in health. To stand by and witness this, and not dare to remonstrate, was a pain no words can render." In exploring the currency of the word "ruth," I could not resist giving Charlotte's description of Emily's last days. On the one hand, how wonderful to have as a witness such a gifted writer as Charlotte Brontë to render the scene; on the other, Charlotte was a fiction writer and might instinctively embellish. Of course we have nothing directly from Emily, except poems that reveal what her own mortality meant to her, which will be discussed in the chapters "Imagination" and "Spirituality." A last thought about the word "ruth." It is perfectly modern when the suffix is added to denote its opposite, "ruthless."

"Thou standest in the greenwood now
The place, the hour the same —
And here the fresh leaves gleam and glow
And there, down in the lake below,
The tiny ripples flame.

"The breeze sings like a summer breeze
Should sing in summer skies
And tower-like rocks and tent-like trees
In mingled glory rise.

"But where is he to-day, to-day?"
"O question not with me."
"I will not, Lady; only say
Where may thy lover be?

"Is he upon some distant shore
Or is he on the sea
Or is the heart thou dost adore
A faithless heart to thee?

"The heart I love, whate'er betide,
Is faithful as the grave
And neither foreign lands divide
Nor yet the rolling wave."

"Then why should sorrow cloud that brow
And tears those yes bedim?
Reply this once — is it that thou
Hast faithless been to him?"

"I gazed upon the cloudless moon
And loved her all the night
Till morning came and ardent noon,
Then I forgot her light —

No — not forgot — eternally
Remains its memory dear;
But could the day seem dark to me
Because the night was fair?

"I well may mourn that only one
Can light my future sky
Even though by such a radiant sun
My moon of life must die."

"'Thou standest in the greenwood now'" presents a conversation between two speakers, one of whom is the "Lady" who explains how she has come to replace her former lover with a new one. The first lover is not at fault; he is faithful, and losing him saddens her. However, the new one simply has greater charms. Brontë's female speaker compares her old love to the moon, and the new one to the sun. She almost pleads, "How can I help it," when she queries, "But could the day seem dark to me / Because the night was fair?" The opening lines point to a place where the Lady at one time appeared with her first lover, which provokes the other voice to question the Lady about her current feelings for her absent one-time beloved. Who is speaking of the two voices is clear except at one point. At the end of the fourth stanza there should be closed quotation marks, indicating the end of the first speaker's dialogue, since the next stanza starts with the second speaker, the Lady.

> **Come, walk with me;**
> There's only thee
> To bless my spirit now;
> We used to love on winter nights
> To wander through the snow.
> Can we not woo back old delights?
> The clouds rush dark and wild;
> They fleck with shade our mountain heights
> The same as long ago,
> And on the horizon rest at last
> In looming masses piled;
> While moonbeams flash and fly so fast
> We scarce can say they smiled.
>
> Come walk with me — come, walk with me;
> We were not once so few;
> But Death has stolen our company
> As sunshine steals the dew:
> He took them one by one, and we
> Are left the only two;

So closer would my feelings twine
Because they have no stay but thine.

"Nay, call me not; it may not be;
Is human love so true?
Can Friendship's flower droop on for years
And then revive anew?
No; though the soil be wet with tears,
How fair so'er it grew;
The vital sap once perished
Will never flow again;
And surer than that dwelling dread,
The narrow dungeon of the dead,
Time parts the hearts of men."

"Come walk with me" is another conversation poem; this time
the genders and identities of the two speakers are not apparent.
The question in this poem is whether love can be revived after
years of separation, particularly when circumstances conspire in
favor. The first voice encourages the other persona to "woo back
old delights" and uses the image of a needy vine to justify that
suggestion: "So closer would my feelings twine / Because they
have no stay but thine." The other speaker is of a different mind:
once over and done, there is no going back because more than
death, time wears out affection, "Time parts the hearts of men."
The question whether time does indeed have the power to quell
affection, particularly in the situation of a beloved's death,
centers the following poem, "Cold in the earth." One parting
thought on this poem. Who am I to question Emily Brontë's
similes; however, the comparison of death to sunshine in the
lines, "But Death has stolen our company / As sunshine steals the
dew" has always bothered me in associating death with the sun,
and I would particularly like to change it because otherwise this
is one of my favorite poems. I wonder if any other reader has had
the same reaction.

Cold in the earth, and the deep snow piled above thee!
Far, far removed, cold in the dreary grave!
Have I forgot, my only Love, to love thee,
Severed at last by Time's all-wearing wave?

Now, when alone, do my thoughts no longer hover
Over the mountains on Angora's shore;
Resting their wings where heath and fern-leaves cover
That noble heart for ever, ever more?

Cold in the earth, and fifteen wild Decembers
From those brown hills have melted into spring —
Faithful, indeed, is the spirit that remembers
After such years of change and suffering!

Sweet Love of youth, forgive if I forget thee
While the World's tide is bearing me along;
Sterner desires and darker hopes beset me,
Hopes which obscure but cannot do thee wrong.

No other Sun has lightened up my heaven;
No other Star has ever shone for me:
All my life's bliss from thy dear life was given —
All my life's bliss is in the grave with thee.

But when the days of golden dreams had perished
And even Despair was powerless to destroy,
Then did I learn how existence could be cherished,
Strengthened and fed without the aid of joy;

Then did I check my tears of useless passion,
Weaned my young soul from yearning after thine;
Sternly denied its burning wish to hasten
Down to that tomb already more than mine!

And even yet, I dare not let it languish,
Dare not indulge in Memory's rapturous pain;
Once drinking deep of that divinest anguish,
How could I seek the empty world again?

"Cold in the earth, and the deep snow piled above thee!" is the
only poem in this chapter that explicitly presents unwanted
death as ending a relationship; the poem "If grief for grief can
touch thee" might feature death in that role as well, but as noted
above, only given one interpretation of that poem. The last poem
in this chapter involves death, but self-inflicted. There are many
poems in which death severs mortal ties, but they join other
death-centered poems in the chapter "Death." This haunting
monologue explores the process over the years of not forgetting,
but adapting. The speaker in the poem, on one hand, believes
that time must have made inroads to dispel her grief and thinks
that she has forgotten to love the deceased; she even rhetorically
asks forgiveness for forgetting. On the other hand, she has not
forgotten as much as she has learned to adjust to a diminished
life. Then, she realizes that she has neither forgotten nor recon-
ciled herself — Memory at the end defeats Time, and anguish
still overtakes her even after fifteen years. Regardless of the des-
ignation of the speaker as "R. Alcona to J. Brenzaida" (two
Gondal characters), the poem sketches Edgar Linton's attitude in
Wuthering Heights after the death of Catherine. Edgar could be
delivering this monologue. Edgar met Catherine Earnshaw as a
youth. He lingers at her grave every anniversary of her death for
years, yearns to join her, and has had no other love; however, he
too has had hopes to occupy him, in his case for his daughter,
which like those in the poem are "Hopes that obscure but cannot
do thee wrong."

O between distress and pleasure
Fond affection cannot be;
Wretched hearts in vain would treasure
Friendship's joys when others flee.

Well I know thine eye would never
Smile, while mine grieved, willingly;
Yet I know thine eye for ever
Could not weep in sympathy.

Let us part, the time is over
When I thought and felt like thee;
I will be an Ocean rover,
I will sail the desert sea.

Isles there are beyond its billow:
Lands where woe may wander free;
And, beloved, thy midnight pillow
Will be soft unwatched by me.

Not on each returning morrow
When thy heart bounds ardently
Need'st thou then dissemble sorrow,
Marking my despondency.

Day by day some dreary token
Will forsake thy memory
Till at last all old links broken
I shall be a dream to thee.

"O between distress and pleasure" has a title, "Song." It
describes a different kind of break-up from that instigated by an
angry slighted lover. The speaker of the poem solemnly accepts
that the time has come to part company because of a disparity in
shared affection. The speaker proposes the separation, notes the
benefits of parting, and insists that she (the gender is not speci-
fied, but I will assume "she") is ready to move on, yet she evinces
a notable tone of sorrow.

The last stanza, which has the lovely lines describing how love
fades, is directed to the state of mind of her lover — he will for-
get her over time until she seems only a dream to him. She does

not conclude that over time "*thou* shall be a dream to *me.*" Maybe she does not believe — despite her insistence that they should part ways — that time will be effective to loosen her bond to him.

Love is like the wild rose-briar,
Friendship like the holly-tree —
The holly is dark when the rose-briar blooms
But which will bloom most constantly?

The wild rose-briar is sweet in spring,
Its summer blossoms scent the air;
Yet wait till winter comes again
And who will call the wild-briar fair?

Then scorn the silly rose-wreath now
And deck thee with the holly's sheen,
That when December blights thy brow
He still may leave thy garland green.

"Love is like the wild rose-briar" has the title "Love and Friendship" and features an extended simile to describe how friendship trumps love because it is constant and will remain when old age arrives. No other poem compares love and friendship or makes friendship a central topic, although Brontë uses the word "friendship" in some instances in connection with lovers, such in the fourth line of the immediately preceding poem and in the poem "Come walk with me" in the lines, "Can Friendship's flower droop on for years / And then revive anew?" Regarding Brontë, herself, and friendship, the people who could be best described as Brontë's friends were her sisters and the family servants. She did have acquaintances, her father's curate, William Weightman, for example, and Charlotte's friend Ellen Nussey, but they were not her friends. The few times that she was away at a boarding school either as student or teacher did not result in any friendships. In fact, according to Charlotte, Emily was miserable away from home.

Ellen Nussey described Emily, whom she knew from her stays at the parsonage, as being very reserved with anyone outside her family and inseparable from Anne. One can only wonder why she avoided social relationships because biography yields little in the way of direct explanation. Charlotte and Mrs. Gaskell, in her biography of Charlotte, described Haworth as a remote outpost devoid of society. That description exaggerates the isolation, so the location of her home does not fully explain her reclusiveness. What makes the most sense is that her life was full enough in its own way. She did have the company of at least one of her sisters throughout her life, with very brief exceptions. Also she had her Gondal creations and the residents of Thrushcross Grange and Wuthering Heights as company. In addition, plot lines, poetic strains, refrains, and metaphors must have been jostling for attention. Genius alone might not create a recluse, but literary genius and irrepressible imagination seem to explain best Emily Brontë's separateness.

Light up thy halls! 'Tis closing day;
I'm drear and lone and far away —
Cold blows on my breast, the northwind's bitter sigh,
And oh, my couch is bleak beneath the rainy sky!

Light up thy halls — and think not of me;
That face is absent now, thou hast hated me so to see —
Bright be thine eyes, undimmed their dazzling shine,
For never, never more shall they encounter mine!

The desert moor is dark; there is tempest in the air;
I have breathed my only wish in one last, one burning
    prayer —
A prayer that would come forth although it lingered long;
That set on fire my heart, but froze upon my tongue.

And now, it shall be done before the morning rise:
I will not watch the sun ascend in yonder skies.

One task alone remains — thy pictured face to view;
And then I go to prove if God, at least, be true!

Do I not see thee now? Thy black resplendent hair;
Thy glory-beaming brow, and smile how heavenly fair!
Thine eyes are turned away — those eyes I would not see,
Their dark, their deadly ray, would more than madden me.

There, go, Deceiver, go! My hand is streaming wet;
My heart's blood flows to buy the blessing — To forget!
Oh could that lost heart give back, back again to thine,
One tenth part of the pain that clouds my dark decline!

Oh could I see thy lids weighed down in cheerless woe;
Too full to hide their tears, too stern to overflow;
Oh could I know thy soul with equal grief was torn,
This fate might be endured — this anguish might
    be borne!

How gloomy grows the night! 'Tis Gondal's wind that blows;
I shall not tread again the deep glens where it rose —
I feel it on my face — "Where, wild blast, dost thou roam?
What do we, wanderer, here, so far away from home?

I do not need thy breath to cool my death-cold brow;
But go to that far land, where she is shining now;
Tell Her my latest wish, tell Her my dreary doom;
Say, that *my* pangs are past, but *Hers* are yet to come."

Vain words — vain, frenzied thoughts! No ear can hear
    me call —
Lost in the vacant air my frantic curses fall
And could she see me now, perchance her lip would smile
Would smile in careless pride and utter scorn the while!

And yet, for all her hate, each parting glance would tell
A stronger passion breathed, burned, in this last farewell.

Unconquered in my soul the Tyrant rules me still;
Life bows to my control, but, Love I cannot kill!

"Light up thy halls! 'Tis closing day" relates through the anguished monologue of the speaker how he has been spurned by a heartless woman with whom he is desperately infatuated. Again there are initials indicating who is speaking to whom in the Gondal story: "F. De Samara to A.G.A." The speaker seems to be raging Lear-like on the moors on a dark and tempestuous night. He stabs himself and tells the wind what he would like for the woman to hear. He takes some small satisfaction in thinking that she will feel some anguish in her life. However much he denigrates her, in his final breath he acknowledges that he loves her still. He would rather die rather than continue to live without her. This poem counts the last of the ways to end a romance, with an extreme version of a break-up and a different perspective on the role death can play in ending a relationship.

CHAPTER FIVE

Death

The predominant topic in the poetry of Emily Brontë would have to be death, just as death is central to *Wuthering Heights*. That assertion regarding *Wuthering Heights* might not be self-evident, but one need only consider the following. In the novel, twelve characters die; although the story is a family saga and deaths in one generation to usher in the next would be natural, twelve is a large number. Not only does death advance the plot, it also defines in large part many of the characters. For example, Nelly Dean is one of those characters whose personalities are influenced or fixed by their perceptions of and reactions to death. She finds death as peace and repose and thus does not fear death. Her attitude comes in handy, since she must attend to several corpses. She believes in heaven, as she tells Lockwood, and wonders if people like Catherine and Heathcliff could be happy there. Nelly's most sorrowful reaction to death comes from Hindley's demise, showing the importance of childhood and pity in mourning: she is particularly affected by his end because she had known him since childhood and pitied him for his shattered life. Catherine, before she dies, takes the opportunity in her brain fever induced rambling to reflect on death and how she considers it freedom and a return to nature, furthering the idea that death is neither heaven nor the end, but liberation from the bonds of life. She also sees her death as a way of punishing Edgar for neglecting her. Hindley, Edgar, and Heathcliff are all set on their course by the death of a loved one. Hareton's earnest grief at the death of Heathcliff shows his personality to be one capable of strong and affectionate attachment; that reaction also reinforces the idea that associations formed in childhood are the strongest because Heathcliff has taken charge of

Hareton since he was a little boy, and Hareton does not realize that Heathcliff's good humor towards him was actually calculated neglect. Heathcliff has a strong belief that death is not the end, although that faith seems to spring from his inability to accept that Catherine is gone. He believes in ghosts and spends years seeking her spirit and preparing to join her — hence the scene of Heathcliff dashing into the bedroom and calling out to Catherine when Lockwood cries out after his nightmare. That scene is just the introduction to his grief; there are many others full of poetic language about how the whole world is a dreadful memoranda that she did exist and that he has lost her, and how he will win his beloved again. The various discussions by Nelly about what awaits Heathcliff and Catherine after death, and Heathcliff's insistence that he will rejoin Catherine, prepare the way at the end of the book for the superstitious belief held among the inhabitants of the environs that the ghosts of Heathcliff and Catherine roam the moors.

In addition to defining character, the centrality of death is also expressed through numeric symbolism. Brontë repeatedly and markedly uses the numbers twelve and two throughout the novel as numeric symbols of death. The symbolic value of the number twelve is easily understandable, given that twelve is the ultimate number for the day and the year. As for the number two, pairs of things — two candles, two lambs, two trees etc. — also appear in an astonishing number, particularly in scenes devoted to thoughts of death or where a death occurs.

In her poetry, Brontë explores death from diverse perspectives. There are poems that describe a dread of death or a wish for death; others weigh and debate the advantages of dying versus living. Poems addressing the aftermath of death analyze grief, frequently depicting that grief leads to despair, such as in the poem "Death that struck when I was most confiding," which makes the point that many sorrows can be overcome, but not grief. Those poems could find a place in the chapter "Hope and Despair" where the causes and nature of despair are chief concerns, but they are included in this chapter because the despair depicted in these poems results from grief alone.

Why would death occupy Brontë's mind and work to such a large extent? From a Gondal standpoint, death figured as a plot incident and she made use of her Gondal characters to present the emotions arising at the prospect of death and from sorrow; however, there are many death-oriented poems that are not Gondal poems. And that answer begs the question, since she might have planned a lot of Gondal deaths in order to explore the topic, rather than vice versa. Perhaps a biographical approach helps answer the question. Death was a more frequent occurrence in Brontë's time than it is now, at least in the Western world. By the time she was twenty-five, Brontë had experienced the deaths of her mother, her two oldest sisters, the family friends, Martha Taylor and William Weightman, and her aunt Branwell, who lived at the parsonage. Life in Haworth at the time was particularly tenuous, as beset by pestilence as the most sordid slums of London.[1] The average life expectancy in Haworth was 25.8 years.[2] Mr. Brontë routinely attended the dying and officiated at funerals and the front yard of her home served as the cemetery, filled to beyond capacity. Young people and children were not strangers to death: Emily and her brother, Branwell, collaborated on a poem as teenagers in which a little girl looks upon the corpse of her sister and imagines how alive she stills seems.

Today, such a poem and pondering death at such length and in such a way appear morbid or unhealthy and certainly taboo for children. Still, the ubiquity of death only explains in part Emily's focus on the topic because neither Charlotte nor Anne devoted herself to exploring it in her writing. Although Brontë could appear obsessed with death, that interest does not necessarily mean that thoughts of her own demise preoccupied her. When she speculated in a brief "diary paper," dated July 30, 1845, to be read three years later, about what the future might hold for her and her sister Anne, she does not intimate that there is any chance that they

---

[1] Ann Dinsdale, *The Brontës at Haworth* (London: Frances Lincoln Ltd, 2006), 119.
[2] Ibid.

would not be alive at that future date. Incidentally, Anne's paper states, "I wonder how we shall all be, and where and how situated on the thirtieth of July 1848." By that date, neither Emily nor Anne was alive, Emily having died in December and Anne in May of that year.

There is another biographical basis for her marked concern with death. As mentioned in the biographical discussion at the beginning of this book, Emily Brontë was not traditionally religious, like Charlotte and Anne. One need only compare the presentation of religion in *Jane Eyre* to that in *Wuthering Heights* to appreciate the differences between Charlotte and Emily in religious matters. *Jane Eyre* no doubt has psychological insights ahead of its time, but in the end, down to the last word "Jesus" it is a staunchly Christian book. Charlotte and Anne, like their father, looked to their religion for consolation, support, and the way to understand death. Branwell, her brother, seemed to have abandoned religion, but in his final moments uttered an "amen" that gave tremendous reassurance to Mr. Brontë that his son was not dying bereft of the support of God. Emily seemed bent on figuring matters out for herself.

Perhaps Brontë's desire to understand death and to reconcile herself to it led her to write poetry as her method for doing so. Conversely, one might conclude that because she had a poetic proclivity she contemplated death, which is certainly an inherently poetic topic. Years after Emily Brontë, Algernon Charles Swinburne wrote in a poem entitled "Ave Atque Vale" that death could not be understood through poetry: "There is no help for these things, none to mend / And none to mar; not all our songs, O friend, / Will make death clear or make life durable." That serves as a general truth, but Emily Brontë, markedly different from the norm, made death clear and life durable for herself through her poetry. I will address her solution in the chapter "Imagination."

I'll come when thou art saddest,
Laid alone in the darkened room;
When the mad day's mirth has vanished,

And the smile of joy is banished
From evening's chilly gloom.

I'll come when the heart's real feeling
Has entire unbiassed sway,
And my influence o'er thee stealing,
Grief deepening, joy congealing,
Shall bear thy soul away.

Listen,'tis just the hour,
The awful time for thee;
Dost thou not feel upon thy soul
A flood of strange sensations roll,
Forerunners of a sterner power,
Heralds of me?

"I'll come when thou art saddest" is in the tradition of a dramatic monologue, and the persona speaking oozes a sinister tone. Not until the end of the poem do we fully understand that the creepy and haughty voice belongs to Death. I have mentioned Brontë's negative capability —to be in the mind of other people and things. Now we have her imagining the perspective of Death. Among the various views of death that Brontë presents, this poem obviously depicts death as dreadful — or in the words of the poem an "awful time." That same adjective is used to describe death in *Wuthering Heights* by Nelly Dean upon seeing Heathcliff's body: "I was stunned by the awful event; and my memory unavoidably recurred to former times with a sort of oppressive sadness." This poem is not the only instance of Brontë personifying death. Although I have stated that she wrote nothing other than *Wuthering Heights* and poetry, small exceptions exist: a few brief notes and her homework exercises written in French while studying in Brussels at the Pensionnat Heger. For one assignment Brontë wrote a piece called "The Palace of Death," in which Death surveys all the evils of the world to select her right-hand man. I have translated and included that essay in the Appendix at the end

of this book, and you can find out which personified evil Death
selects.

Methinks this heart should rest awhile,
So stilly round the evening falls;
The veiled sun sheds no parting smile,
Nor mirth, nor music wakes my halls.

I have sat lonely all the day
Watching the drizzly mist descend
And first conceal the hills in grey
And then along the valleys wend.

And I have sat and watched the trees
And the sad flowers — how drear they blow:
Those flowers were formed to feel the breeze
Wave their light leaves in summer's glow.

Yet their lives passed in gloomy woe
And hopeless comes its dark decline,
And I lament, because I know
That cold departure pictures mine.

"Methinks this heart should rest awhile" depicts death not as
terrifying and awful, but dark and gloomy, though entirely in the
nature of things. Death is as unwelcome as the blight and darkness
of winter, and the death of the flowers mirrors the natural and
eventual end of the speaker. In contrast to the predominate idea in
the poems in the chapter "Nature," this poem does not present
nature as a consoling power, but as a *momento mori*.

The evening passes fast away,
'Tis almost time to rest;
What thoughts has left the vanished day?
What feelings in thy breast?

"The vanished day? It leaves a sense
Of labour hardly done;
Of little gained with vast expense —
A sense of grief alone!

"Time stands before the door of Death,
Upbraiding bitterly;
And Conscience, with exhaustless breath,
Pours black reproach on me:

"And though I think that Conscience lies,
And Time should Fate condemn;
Still, weak Repentance clouds my eyes,
And makes me yield to them!"

Then art thou glad to seek repose?
Art glad to leave the sea,
And anchor all thy weary woes
In calm Eternity?

Nothing regrets to see thee go —
Not one voice sobs, "Farewell";
And where thy heart has suffered so
Canst thou desire to dwell?

"Alas! the countless links are strong
That bind us to our clay;
The loving spirit lingers long,
And would not pass away —

"And rest is sweet, when laurelled fame
Will crown the soldier's crest;
But a brave heart with a tarnished name,
Would rather fight than rest."

Well, thou hast fought for many a year,
Hast fought thy whole life through,
Hast humbled Falsehood, trampled Fear;
What is there left to do?

"'Tis true, this arm has hotly striven,
Has dared what few would dare;
Much have I done, and freely given,
But little learnt to bear!"

Look on the grave where thou must sleep,
Thy last, and strongest foe;
'Twill be endurance not to weep,
If that repose seem woe.

The long fight closing in defeat —
Defeat serenely borne —
Thine eventide may still be sweet,
Thy night a glorious morn.

"The evening passes fast away" analyzes the emotions of a person facing death through a dialogue between that person and a disembodied voice or perhaps simply with himself taking the other side of the question. Although it is not clear why, the time has come for this person to depart life and the question is not whether he should chose life or death but rather whether he can bring himself to find his death welcome. One of the eternal questions figures here: why dread death when life has been fraught with suffering. One answer, provided here, is simply that the links that bind us to life are strong and, if there has been anything to love, one would cling to that. Further, the speaker offers as an excuse for his unwillingness to accept death that he has not accomplished enough — with his tarnished name, he would rather carry on than rest. Impending death in this poem is established through metaphor: the evening passing fast away and leaving the sea to seek repose are phrases indicating the end of life. Even the martial reference could be metaphorical — he was not literally a soldier, but one who has contended with the shortcomings of life: lies and fear. The slightly hopeful tone at the end suggests that evening might be sweet after all and night a glorious morn. In the metaphorical context of the poem, that means that the final hours, if acceptance is achieved, could be sweet, and his death a new beginning — which interpretation makes sense of the paradox that night is morning, since the end of life (night) is a new beginning (morn) of eternity.

In the earth, the earth, thou shalt be laid,
A grey stone standing over thee;
Black mould beneath thee spread
And black mould to cover thee.

"Well, there is rest there,
So fast come thy prophecy;
The time when my sunny hair
Shall with grass roots entwinèd be."

But cold, cold is that resting-place,
Shut out from Joy and Liberty,
And all who loved thy living face
Will shrink from its gloom and thee.

"Not so: *here* the world is chill,
And sworn friends fall from me;
But *there,* they will own me still
And prize my memory."

Farewell, then, all that love,
All that deep sympathy:
Sleep on; heaven laughs above,
Earth never misses thee.

Turf-sod and tombstone drear
Part human company;

One heart breaks only there —
That heart was worthy thee!

"In the earth, the earth, thou shalt be laid" treats the same question as the poem immediately above — is death dreadful or welcome; however, it veers into a more cynical outcome in considering that the eternal resting place is cold and that the deceased's survivors will shrink from his corpse and over time forsake his memory. The last two lines are enigmatic in professing that only one heart would be saddened by his passing — whose heart? Is there, perhaps, a story line underlying this poem in which figures one true friend? Alternatively, it could be that only *his* heart would break and he was worthy of such a noble heart. The quotation marks make the change in speakers clear: the words of the first voice to speak, the one who sees no benefit in death, are not quoted; the speaker who has found the world lacking and thinks that death will have advantages is within quotes. We do not know if the second speaker is convinced by the arguments of the other; however, since the first speaker gets the last word, from a thematic standpoint, the argument seems resolved in favor of that speaker's position, i.e. that life is preferable to death.

A thousand sounds of happiness,
And only one of real distress,
One hardly uttered groan —
But that has hushed all vocal joy,
Eclipsed the glory of the sky,
And made me think that misery
Rules in our world alone!

About his face the sunshine glows,
And in his hair the south wind blows,
And violet and wild wood-rose
Are sweetly breathing near;
Nothing without suggests dismay,
If he could force his mind away

From tracking father, day by day,
The desert of Despair.

Too truly agonized to weep,
His eyes are motionless as sleep;
His frequent sighs, long-drawn and deep,
Are anguish to my ear;
And I would soothe — but can I call
The cold corpse from its funeral pall,
And cause a gleam of hope to fall
With my consoling tear?
O Death, so many spirits driven
Through this false world, their all had given
To win the everlasting haven
To sufferers so divine —
Why didst thou smite the loved, the blest,
The ardent and the happy breast,
That, full of hope, desired not rest
And shrank appalled from thine?

At least, since thou wilt not restore,
In mercy, launch one arrow more;
Life's conscious Death it wearies sore,
It tortures worse than thee.
Enough of storms have bowed his head:
Grant him at last a quiet bed,
Beside his early stricken dead —
Even where he years to be!

"A thousand sounds of happiness" supports the idea that death can be preferable to life, in the life versus death debate discussed in the two immediately preceding poems. Here is yet a slightly different perspective; death brings relief to the grief-stricken. The speaker witnesses the suffering of another, one who is overcome with sorrow, and concludes that he would be better off with his beloved in the grave. That notion is of course reminiscent of

Heathcliff who yearns to die, join Catherine, and thereby achieve his heaven. The idea in the first stanza that the suffering of *one* person suffices to eclipse all joy emphasizes the power of grief, like in the poem, "From our evening fireside now," where the death of *one* saddens *all*. Numbers are meaningless where suffering, particularly grief, is concerned. This poem depicts a state of despair, observed and heard, and it is so painful to the speaker of the poem that one might wonder if she (maybe, he) wants to put the mourner out of his misery in part to spare herself — after all, she is the one who feels so helpless to console and who calls death to launch on arrow more. The detailed depiction of despair certainly qualifies this poem for inclusion in the chapter "Hope and Despair," but since it exhibits the despair uniquely caused by grief, the poem has landed here, and will be joined by several others making the same point that grief equals despair. On another note, the image of death as an archer is worth considering. It subverts the image from Greek mythology of Eros (or Cupid), who shoots arrows causing infatuation, but it also resembles the Niobe myth in which Apollo and Artemis shoot arrows at and kill all fourteen of Niobe's children. Also, the archer as death fits the image of death in the next poem as a force that strikes.

Death, that struck when I was most confiding
In my certain Faith of Joy to be,
Strike again, Time's withered branch dividing
From the fresh root of Eternity!

Leaves, upon Time's branch, were growing brightly,
Full of sap, and full of silver dew;
Birds beneath its shelter gathered nightly;
Daily, round its flowers, the wild bees flew.

Sorrow passed and plucked the golden blossom,
Guilt stripped off the foliage in its pride;
But, within its parent's kindly bosom,
Flowed forever Life's restoring tide.

Little mourned I for the parted Gladness,
For the vacant nest and silent song;
Hope was there, and laughed me out of sadness;
Whispering, "Winter will not linger long."

And, behold, with tenfold increase blessing
Spring adorned the beauty-burdened spray;
Wind and rain and fervent heat, caressing
Lavished glory on its second May.

High it rose; no winged grief could sweep it;
Sin was scared to distance with its shine:
Love and its own life had power to keep it
From all wrong, from every blight but thine!

Heartless Death, the young leaves droop and languish!
Evening's gentle air may still restore —
No: the morning sunshine mocks my anguish —
Time for me must never blossom more!

Strike it down, that other boughs may flourish
Where that perished sapling used to be;
Thus, at least, its mouldering corpse will nourish
That from which it sprung — Eternity.

"Death, that struck when I was most confiding" furthers the
idea in the previous poem that grief leads to despair and a desire
for death. The structure of the poem consists of an introductory
stanza that will be echoed at the conclusion. After the first stanza,
the narrative goes back in time and then moves chronologically
to the event that constitutes the terminal blow. Through the
flashback, we see that the young tree (a "sapling") has recovered
from various vicissitudes, buoyed by Hope. Then "Heartless
Death" strikes, bringing us up to the time of the first and last
stanzas in which the speaker asks for death to strike her. There is
a curious reverse personification in this poem. Instead of person-

ifying an object by giving it human qualities, Brontë gives a person, the speaker of the poem, the qualities of a non-human thing
— a tree.

One of the branches is "Time's branch," the part of the tree that seems most representative of human existence. The roots of the tree, the soul, will never die, but remain as part of eternity. She calls out for Death to strike again — to strike her, since "Time for me will never blossom more."

Grief has caused hopelessness that can only be remedied by quitting life. The end of the poem offers a view of death as a natural process and the consoling concept of eternity, an idea that encompasses where the tree / the speaker came from and to where it /she will return.

> **The day is done, the winter sun**
> Is setting in its sullen sky;
> And drear the course that has been run,
> And dim the hearts that slowly die.
>
> No star will light my coming night;
> No morn of hope for me will shine;
> I mourn not heaven would blast my sight,
> And I ne'er longed for ways divine.
>
> Through Life hard Task I did not ask
> Celestial aid, celestial cheer;
> I saw my fate without its mask,
> And met it too without a tear.
>
> The grief that pressed this living breast
> Was heavier far than earth can be;
> And who would dread eternal rest
> When labour's hour was agony?
>
> Dark falls the fear of this despair
> On spirits born of happiness;

But I was bred the mate of care,
The foster-child of sore distress.

No sighs for me, no sympathy,
No wish to keep my soul below;
The heart is dead since infancy,
Unwept-for let the body go.

"The Day is done, the winter sun" bears the title, "Castle Wood," and presents a Gondal character expressing the same thought as in the previous poems: death is preferable to a life of grief. In the life versus death debate, the speaker in this poem unequivocally wishes to die because the despair resulting from grief has augmented the distress and agony that has monopolized life, at least since childhood. Death appeals to the speaker because it will bring relief and constitutes only a loss of the corporeal frame, as suggested by the words "let the body go"; however, contrary to other poems weighing life against death, no glorious morn or blissful eternity graces the speaker's perception of death to blunt its finality. Incidentally, I paused at the phrase, "I saw my fate without its mask," not only because it is a striking image for the idea of facing life, but also because it reminded me of the anecdote famous in Brontë lore regarding masks. Mr. Brontë, wanting to discover his little children's intellects had each in turn wear a mask, thinking, with psychological perspicacity, that under a mask they would speak more freely. He posed a different question for each, to which the children (five of them at the time) gave not only well considered and rather precocious answers, but also responses that revealed the personalities of each.

I die; but when the grave shall press
The heart so long endeared to thee,
When earthly cares no more distress
And earthly joys are nought to me,

Weep not, but think that I have past
Before thee o'er a sea of gloom,
Have anchored safe and rest at last
Where tears and mourning cannot come.

'Tis I should weep to leave thee here,
On the dark Ocean, sailing drear,
With storms around and fears before
And no kind light to point the shore.

But long or short though life may be
'Tis nothing to eternity;
We part below to meet on high
Where blissful ages never die.

"I die; but when the grave shall press" is entitled "Lines" and
also weighs the benefits of death over life; death trumps life
because life is dreary and distressing and death offers a safe harbor
where tears and mourning are absent in a blissful eternity. The
metaphor of an ocean or sea and sailing on it to represent the world
and living recurs in many poems, just as reaching the shore or port
means dying. The situation in which the words are spoken distin-
guishes this poem from the foregoing and perhaps makes a
difference to the conclusion: on the topic of whether it is best to
die, the speaker is neither mulling things over to herself, nor is
someone commenting on her state of despair, nor is she having a
debate with another voice on the befits of life versus death. The
speaker addresses the loved ones who will survive her and tries to
console them — does that context explain perhaps the conclusion
that a blissful eternity awaits?

Sleep brings no joy to me,
Remembrance never dies;
My soul is given to misery,
And lives in sighs.

Sleep brings no rest to me;
The shadows of the dead
My wakening eyes may never see,
Surround my bed.

Sleep brings no hope to me;
In soundest sleep they come,
And with their doleful imagery
Deepen the gloom.

Sleep brings no strength to me,
No power renewed to brave:
I only sail a wilder sea,
A darker wave.

Sleep brings no friend to me
To soothe and aid to bear;
They all gaze, oh, how scornfully!
And I despair.

Sleep brings no wish to knit
My harassed heart beneath;
My only wish is to forget
In sleep of death.

"Sleep brings no joy to me" focuses on one new element of grief, the futility of sleep to bring relief, and one recurrent idea, that grief can be assuaged only by death. The speaker in the poem concludes that there is no escape from the relentless, obtrusive thoughts except by dying, so it is her wish to die. There is a progression through three phases pertaining to sleep. At first thoughts of the dead prevent the speaker from resting; the third stanza clarifies that even in deep sleep thoughts of the departed obtrude. Last, upon waking there is no gain in strength or calm. The poem is designated, "A.G.A.", the initials of the Augusta from Gondal who appears frequently in the Gondal poems. Who she is mourning? It seems like there are several, since she refers to "shadows of the dead." In any event, their identities are not important to appreciating the poem and its statement about the inescapability of grief. The connection of sleep to escape, which is so soundly denied in this poem, also appears in John Keats's sonnet "To Sleep." By contrast, in that poem Keats summons sleep as a savior in the form of a warder who will arrive with his ring of keys to lock the soul from painful, plaguing thoughts: "Turn the key deftly in the oiled wards, / And seal the hushed Casket of my Soul." However, maybe the two poems actually intersect at the point of "the sleep of death." Brontë's poem recommends death as the only consoling kind of sleep, and Keats imbues his poem with images of death suggesting sleep has death-like properties or is even a metaphor for death.

From our evening fireside now,
Merry laugh and cheerful tone,
Smiling eye and cloudless brow,
Mirth and music, all are flown;

Yet the grass before the door
Grows as green in April rain;
And as blithely as of yore
Larks have poured their day-long strain.

Is it fear or is it sorrow
Checks the stagnant stream of joy?
Do we tremble that to-morrow
May some future peace destroy?

For past misery are we weeping?
What is past can hurt no more;
And the gracious heavens are keeping
Aid for that which lies before.

One is absent, and for one
Cheerless, chill is our hearthstone.
One is absent, and for him
Cheeks are pale and eyes are dim.

Arthur, brother, Gondal's shore
Rested from the battles roar —
Arthur, brother, we returned
Back to Desmond lost and mourned.

Thou didn't purchase by thy fall
Home for us and peace for all;
Yet, how darkly dawned that day —
Dreadful was the price to pay!

Just as once, through sun and mist
I have climbed the mountain's breast;
Still my gun, with certain aim
Brought to earth the fluttering game;

But the very dogs repined;
Though I called with whistle shrill,
Listlessly they lagged behind,
Looking backward o'er the hill.

Sorrow was not vocal there;
Mute their pain and my despair;
But the joy of life was flown:
He was gone and we were lone.

So it is by morn and eve —
So it is in field and hall:
For the absent one we grieve,
One being absent saddens All.

"From our evening fireside now" mourns the loss of a soldier. There is a designation that the poem is "By R. Gleneden," a Gondal character, who apparently is a poet, as these lines are by him. The poem imparts in word and image a true sense of what it means to mourn. Sadness pervades all, and the carefree beauty of nature seems out of place. Further, the narrator describes two situations that should be enjoyable for him (a cozy evening by the fireside and hunting birds on the mountain) but that are devoid of any joy because Arthur, his brother, has not returned alive. Regardless of the fictional nature of the battle, this poem captures a sentiment that qualifies it as a lament for the fallen with its lines, "Thou dids't purchase by thy fall / Home for us and peace for all; Yet how darkly dawned that day— / Dreadful was the price to pay!" The poem also attacks the concept of an acceptable number of casualties, when it insists "*One* being absent saddens All."

The busy day has hurried by,
And hearts greet kindred hearts once more;
And swift the evening hours should fly,
But — what turns every gleaming eye
So often to the door,

And then so quick away — and why
Does sudden silence chill the room,
And laughter sink into a sigh,
And merry words to whispers die,
And gladness change to gloom?

O we are listening for a sound
We know shall ne'er be heard again;
Sweet voices in the halls resound,
Fair forms, fond faces gather round,
But all in vain — in vain!

Their feet shall never waken more
The echoes in these galleries wide,

Nor dare the snow on the mountain's brow,
Nor skim the river's frozen flow,
Nor wander down its side.

They who have been our life — our soul —
Through summer-youth, from childhood's spring —
Who bound us in one vigorous whole
To stand 'gainst Tyranny's control
For ever triumphing —

Who bore the brunt of battle's fray:
The first to fight, the last to fall;
Whose mighty minds, with kindred ray,
Still led the van in Glory's way,
The idol chiefs of all —

They, they are gone! Not for a while
As golden suns at night decline
And even in death our grief beguile
Foretelling, with a rose-red smile,
How bright the morn will shine.

No; these dark towers are lone and lorn;
This very crowd is vacancy;
And we must watch and wait and mourn
And half look out for their return,
And think their forms we see;

And fancy music in our ear,
Such as their lips could only pour;
And think we feel their presence near,
And start to find they are not here,
And never shall be more!

"The busy day has hurried by" shows Brontë's careful observation of or experience with grief and what a powerful poem it is. I have mentioned in other contexts that her imagination compensated for a lack of actual experience, yet we know that she had opportunities to experience grief. However, whether she is mining her own memory or creating, she vividly renders a series of sensations attending grief: the momentary forgetting, expectation, and incredulity. Sight, sound and the tactile sense are all implicated, and pleasure, even from normally enjoyable situations, is vanquished. I particularly find that the line "This very crowd is vacancy" hits the target. Like the previous poem, the deceased (more than one in this case) have lost their lives in battle. This poem even more than any others that deal with life lost in battle offers apt expressions for Memorial Day: "Who bore the brunt of battle's fray; / The first to fight, the last to fall; / Whose mighty minds, with kindred ray, / Still led the van in Glory's way."

"The winter wind is loud and wild;
Come close to me, my darling child!
Forsake thy books, and mateless play;
And, while the night is gathering grey,
We'll talk its pensive hours away —

"Iernë, round our sheltered hall,
November's gusts unheeded call;
Not one faint breath can enter here
Enough to wave my daughter's hair;

"And I am glad to watch the blaze
Glance from her eyes, with mimic rays;
To feel her cheek, so softly pressed
In happy quiet on my breast;

"But, yet, even this tranquillity
Brings bitter, restless thoughts to me;
And, in the red fire's cheerful glow,
I think of deep glens, blocked with snow;

"I dream of moor, and misty hill,
Where evening gathers dark and chill,
For, lone, among the mountains cold
Lie those that I have loved of old,
And my heart aches, in hopeless pain,
Exhausted with repinings vain,
That I shall greet them ne'er again!"

"Father, in early infancy,
When you were far beyond the sea,
Such thoughts were tyrants over me —
I often sat, for hours together,
Through the long nights of angry weather,
Raised on my pillow, to descry
The dim moon struggling in the sky;
Or, with strained ear, to catch the shock,
Of rock with wave, and wave with rock.
So would I fearful vigil keep,
And, all for listening, never sleep;
But this world's life has much to dread:
Not so, my Father, with the Dead.

"O not for them, should we despair;
The grave is drear, but they are not there:
Their dust is mingled with the sod;
Their happy souls are gone to God!
You told me this, and yet you sigh,
And murmur that your friends must die.
Ah, my dear father, tell me why?

"For, if your former words were true,
How useless would such sorrow be!
As wise to mourn the seed which grew
Unnoticed on its parent tree,

"Because it fell in fertile earth
And sprang up to a glorious birth —
Struck deep its roots, and lifted high
Its green boughs in the breezy sky!

"But, I'll not fear — I will not weep
For those whose bodies lie asleep:
I know there is a blessed shore
Opening its ports for me and mine;
And, gazing Time's wide waters o'er,
I weary for that land divine,

"Where we were born — where you and I
Shall meet our dearest, when we die;
From suffering and corruption free,
Restored into the Deity."

"Well hast thou spoken, sweet, trustful child!
And wiser than thy sire:
And coming tempests, raging wild,
Shall strengthen thy desire —
Thy fervent hope, through storm and foam,
Through wind and ocean's roar,
To reach, at last, the eternal home —
The steadfast, changeless shore!"

"'The Winter wind is loud and wild'" presents a debate about grief. In the same vein as other poems that ask why dread death if there is a glorious hereafter, this one queries why grieve if one believes that the departed are happy in eternity. The identity of the two speakers is important: the first to speak is the "Father," the wiser one presumably, who has taught his daughter, Irenë, the other speaker, that the departed are happily gone to God and there is no need to mourn. Another salient aspect of his identity is that he is older and has had experiences that still await his daughter. In the current time frame of their conversation, he laments what has passed, expressing ideas akin to those in the poems in the chapter "Mutability." Echoing those poems, there is no particular reason his thoughts turn to the past, in particular to those who have died, other than the sound of the wind and autumn's gloom; there has not occurred any particular death recently that he is mourning, as in the poems above. Despite the mutability-related sentiments of nostalgia, this poem features grief predominantly and explores whether belief serves as consolation for grief. His daughter, a child, reminds him that the dead are at peace, reciting what she has learned from him. In the daughter's rebuttal, she speaks of a tree and a seed dropping from it to spring into the earth, recalling the metaphor of a tree in the poem "Death that struck when I was most confiding." The trope in this poem suggests that the seed dropping into the earth and flourishing constitutes dying and achieving eternity. The father commends her on being right, but his final words intimate that he believes that she is able to feel so tranquil and certain only because she is young. Despite his admission that she is correct in not mourning, his mood does not improve, as shown by his final foreboding words that she will need her beliefs to withstand what life will bring. Retuning for a moment to the Father's sadness for those whom he has loved of old, Byron voiced a comparable sentiment in "Childe Harold" when he wrote, "What is the worst of woes that wait on age? / What stamps the wrinkle deeper on the brow? / To view each loved one blotted from life's page, / And be alone on earth, as I am now."

CHAPTER SIX

Captivity and Freedom

Captivity and freedom figure largely as topics in Emily Brontë's writing in both a literal and figurative way. In *Wuthering Heights* characters suffer actual confinement as well as a figurative imprisonment by earthly existence and gain freedom by escape or by dying, as the case may be. The most salient literal imprisonment occurs when Heathcliff detains Catherine (the younger) and Nelly Dean at Wuthering Heights to ensure Catherine marries his son Linton and to further torment her and her father. She is again imprisoned at Wuthering Heights after her father dies when Heathcliff forces her to quit Thrushcross Grange and live there. Earlier in the story, she is in a sense captive at Thrushcross Grange and its park, and escapes when she pursues her clandestine relationship with Linton. The snowstorm makes a prisoner of Lockwood during his second visit to *Wuthering Heights*. Isabella makes an escape from Wuthering Heights where she has been imprisoned, running to Thrushcross Grange and then farther away to escape Heathcliff. Linton Heathcliff is a kind of prisoner as well — he is forced away from his uncle's home to live at Wuthering Heights with no ability to escape other than through death. As a boy, Heathcliff is imprisoned by Hindley who locks him up in the garret as punishment and to feed his long-standing hatred of him. From a metaphorical standpoint, the novel presents life as captivity and death as freedom. Catherine expresses that notion during her final bout with brain fever when she says that she is tired of feeling confined and wants to be free. Likewise, death will set Linton Heathcliff free: he will only escape the tyranny of his father, Heathcliff, at death, which he looks forward to. Heathcliff also will escape his tormenting grief by dying. However, death is not the only metaphor for freedom in the novel; the moors are also a symbol of freedom, as the place to which Heathcliff and Catherine escape as children.

In the poems, the dichotomy of literal and figurative presentations of captivity and freedom continues. At times a character in a story poem languishes in a dungeon and freedom is actually gaining release. Other times the imprisonment and freedom are metaphorical and the images of captivity and release represent other situations in life or states of mind. The Gondal story line, which inspires a vast number of Brontë's poems, provides ample opportunity to depict literal dungeons, since the vanquished of the saga's battles would, in keeping with history's example, wind up in a dungeon.

Lord Byron's poem "The Prisoner of Chillon" offers a precedent of a literal dungeon poem. Byron recounts the imprisonment of François Bonivard and his two brothers, inspired by his visit to the Château de Chillon in Montreux, Switzerland and its infamous dungeon. By the way, in Byron's poetic rendering of that historical event, the sole survivor becomes so accustomed to his captivity that when his release comes, he does not want to leave. That is a psychological reaction that Brontë does not impute to any of her characters. Brontë no doubt did read that poem, but there is no knowing whether it influenced her to write her captivity poems. As an aside, regarding Byron, I mention him frequently, at times as a likely influence on Brontë. Indeed, there is collective agreement among the interested that he was a very important influence on the Brontës; for example, both Rochester and Heathcliff are commonly referred to as "Byronic." Here are two trivial tidbits that might indicate how well-known Byron was in the Brontë household: Byron had a love affair with his half-sister, whose name was Augusta; Brontë's creation, Heathcliff, loves his adopted sister, and Brontë's heroine in the Gondal saga is named Augusta. Further, is it coincidence that Anne Brontë named her book about a governess *Agnes Grey* or did she know of Byron's governess, who was named Agnes Gray? The similarities in the poetic works of Brontë and Byron have not eluded scholars, who have identified specific examples of Byron's inspiration on theme, sentiment, and even diction in Brontë's poetry.

Returning to Brontë's rendering of captivity and freedom, some poems suggest a metaphorical more than literal interpretation; being forced to live away from home amongst a crowd is a kind of captivity, and nature, like the moors in *Wuthering Heights*, figures as freedom. Brontë's poems on the subject of captivity and freedom that are entirely metaphorical, featuring, for example, captivity as life and freedom as death, veer into the thematic realms addressed in the chapters "Hope and Despair" and "Spirituality."

O God of heaven! The dream of horror,
The frightful dream is over now;
The sickened heart, the blasting sorrow,
The ghastly night, the ghastlier morrow,
The aching sense of utter woe;

The burning tears that would keep welling,
The groans that mocked at every tear
That burst from out their dreary dwelling
As if each gasp were life expelling,
But life was nourished by despair;

The tossing and the anguished pining;
The grinding teeth and staring eye;
The agony of still repining,
When not a spark of hope was shining
From gloomy fate's relentless sky;

The impatient rage, the useless shrinking
From thoughts that yet could not be borne;
The soul that was for ever thinking,
Till nature, maddened, tortured, sinking,
At last refused to mourn —

It's over now — and I am free,
And the ocean wind is caressing me,
The wild wind from the wavy main
I never thought to see again.

Bless thee, Bright Sea — and glorious dome,
And my own world, my spirit's home;
Bless thee, Bless all — I can not speak:
My voice is choked, but not with grief;
And salt drops from my haggard cheek
Descend, like rain upon the heath.

How long they've wet a dungeon floor,
Falling on flagstones damp and grey!
I used to weep even in my sleep;
The night was dreadful, like the day.

I used to weep when winter's snow
Whirled through the grating stormily;
But then it was a calmer woe,
For everything was drear as me.

The bitterest time, the worst of all,
Was that in which the summer sheen
Cast a green luster on the wall
That told of fields of lovelier green.

Often I've sat down on the ground,
Gazing up to that flush scarce seen,
Till, heedless of the darkness round,
My soul has sought a land serene.

It sought the arch of heaven divine,
The pure blue heaven with clouds of gold;
It sought thy father's home and mine
As I remembered it of old.

Oh, even now too horribly
Come back the feelings that would swell,
When with my face hid on my knee
I strove the bursting groans to quell.

I flung myself upon the stone,
I howled, and tore my tangled hair,
And then, when the first gust had flown,
Lay in unspeakable despair.

Sometimes a curse, sometimes a prayer,
Would quiver on my parchèd tongue;
But both without a murmur there
Died in the breast from whence they sprung.

And so the day would fade on high,
And darkness quench that lonely beam,
And slumber mould my misery
Into some strange and spectral dream,
Whose phantom horrors made me know
The worst extent of human woe —

But this is past, and why return
O'er such a past to brood and mourn?
Shake off the fetters, break the chain,
And live and love and smile again.

The waste of youth, the waste of years,
Departed in that dongeon's thrall;
The gnawing grief, the hopeless tears,
Forget them — O forget them all.

"O God of heaven! The dream of horror" recounts through a
flashback the suffering endured by the speaker while he or she
languished in a dungeon. Even though the dungeon setting would
set up the expectation of a Gondal episode, there is no indication

that it is a Gondal poem. I think this poem invites the interpretation of literal imprisonment, like that of the prisoner of Chillon, Jean Valjean, Edmund Dantès or any other of the many literary or historical figures who have suffered that fate. Also, even though the narrator calls the experience a dream, that term does not suggest that the experience was only a nightmare, but rather relates how such an awful episode appears in hindsight and by contrast to the present state of freedom — the open sky, the breeze, the bright sea, and friendly faces. Despite that conclusion and my general suggestion in the discussion above that certain poems are literal, there is no reason not to indulge a metaphorical interpretation as well — indeed, as a general matter, there is scarcely a limit to metaphorical interpretations of things. The benefit of the metaphorical view is to give the poem meaning, if need be, beyond the idea that prisoners suffer horribly, lose years irretrievably, and might never overcome the dreadful memories.

I know that tonight the wind is sighing,
The soft August wind, over the forest and moor;
While I in a grave-like chill am lying
On the damp black flags of my dungeon-floor.

I know that the Harvest Moon is shining:
She neither will wax nor wane for me;
Yet, I weary, weary with vain repining,
One gleam of her heaven-bright face to see!

For this constant darkness is wasting the gladness,
Fast wasting the gladness of life away:
It gathers up thoughts akin to madness
That never would cloud the world of day.

I chide with my soul — I bid it cherish
The feeling it lived on when I was free,
But shrinking it murmurs, "Let Memory perish,
Forget, for thy friends have forgotten thee!"

Alas, I did think that they were weeping
Such tears as I weep — it is not so!
Their careless young eyes are closed in sleeping;
Their brows are unshadowed, undimmed by woe.

Might I go to their beds, I'd rouse that slumber;
My spirit should startle their rest, and tell
How, hour after hour, I wakefully number
Deep buried from light in my lonely cell!

Yet, let them dream on, though dreary dreaming
Would haunt my pillow if *they* were here,
And *I* were laid warmly under the gleaming
Of that guardian moon and her comrade star.

Better that I, my own fate mourning,
Should pine alone in the prison-gloom,
Than waken free on the summer morning
And feel they were suffering this awful doom.

"I know that tonight the wind is sighing" has the title "M.A. Written on the Dungeon Wall — N.C.," which indicates that it is a Gondal poem. Here, the captive speaks from a dungeon, recounts his or her misery, and expresses the certainty that loved ones have forgotten him (or her). There is no explanation to justify that conclusion expect to infer that he has not received any word from them. In the chapter "Death," poems with lines like "Time parts the hearts of men" and "Turf-sod and tombstone drear / Part human company" mirror the thought in this poem that time erodes affection. Further, with those quoted lines in mind, one can see this poem as featuring an extended metaphor for death — the captive is dead and the survivors have forgotten him. Diction adds to the viability of that interpretation: he imagines his "spirit" visiting the bedside of his loved ones like a spectral haunting; he refers to his cell as having a "grave-like" chill; he describes himself as buried deep from light. Also, in the poem "Come walk with me" Brontë calls a grave "that narrow dungeon of the dead." An interpretation that the dungeon represents death further works because the prisoner never escapes to freedom. If Brontë is using the dungeon as an extended metaphor for death, she is presenting death as the opposite from what she does frequently in this group of poems, as freedom. I find that variety in keeping with her work, as Brontë certainly explored all sides of a topic. Another idea expressed in this poem is that it is better to suffer than know that a loved one suffers. Here, the prisoner would rather languish alone than change places and have to think about a loved one in his situation. That same notion also appears in the poem "May flowers are opening" in the chapter "Hope and Despair." There, the greatest sorrow comes from knowing that loved ones will have to suffer and grieve. These companion expressions about the suffering of others strike me as very Emily Brontëan sentiments because they require two traits native to her world: ruth (to use her word from the poem "If grief for grief can touch thee") and imagination.

> **O transient voyager of heaven!**
> O silent sign of winter skies!
> What adverse wind thy sail has driven
> To dungeons where a prisoner lies?
>
> Methinks the hands that shut the sun
> So sternly from this mourning brow
> Might still their rebel task have done
> And checked a think so frail as thou.
>
> They would have done it had they known
> The talisman that dwelt in thee,
> For all the suns that ever shone
> Have never been so kind to me.
>
> For many a week, and many a day,
> My heart was weighed with sinking gloom,

When morning rose in mourning grey
And faintly lit my prison room;

But, angel like, when I awoke,
Thy silvery form so soft and fair,
Shining through darkness, sweetly spoke
Of cloudy skies and mountains bare —

The dearest to a mountaineer,
Who, all life long has loved the snow
That crowned her native summits drear
Better than the greenest plains below.

And, voiceless, soulless messenger,
Thy presence waked a thrilling tone
That comforts while thou art here
And will sustain when thou art gone.

"O transient voyager of heaven" bears a title, "To a Wreath of
Snow," and is a Gondal poem, attributed to A.G. Almeda. It
begins with an apostrophe to a snowflake that the speaker, a
dungeon prisoner, has surprisingly espied. As a mountain dweller,
seeing snow brings a thrill and comfort. There is no escape to
freedom in this poem, but there is the consolation of catching a
glimpse of the snow. In various poems (whether in this chapter or
in the chapters on nature, mutability, imagination, or spirituality)
an aspect of nature, such as snow, the wind, or the moon, frequently
has the power to console or even to carry the poet or a character
away from earthly confinement. This poem lends itself to a less
literal expression of imprisonment for the following reasons. The
last stanza is akin to the poems discussed in the chapter
"Spirituality" because, as in those poems, a visitant, like the
snowflake, brings a "thrilling tone" and imparts comfort to a trou-
bled soul. Also, a notable difference between this poem and the
previous two dungeon poems is the degree of emotion the captive
demonstrates. Here, in marked contrast to the intense suffering

and woe that fill the previous two poems, the captive only complains, "For many a week, and many a day, / My heart was weighed with sinking gloom," which makes the dungeon seem less forbidding and also less real and less literal.

> "**Listen! When your hair, like mine,**
> Takes a tint of silver grey;
> When your eyes, with dimmer shine,
> Watch life's bubbles float away;

> "When you, young man, have borne like me,
> The weary weight of sixty-three,
> Then shall penance sore be paid
> For these hours so wildly squandered;
> And the words that now fall dead
> On your ears, be deeply pondered;
> Pondered and approved at last,
> But their virtue will be past!

> "Glorious is the prize of Duty,
> Though she be a serious power;
> Treacherous all the lures of Beauty,
> Thorny bud and poisonous flower!

> "Mirth is but a mad beguiling
> Of the golden-gifted Time;
> Love, a demon-meteor, wiling
> Heedless feet to gulfs of crime.

> "Those who follow earthly pleasure,
> Heavenly knowledge will not lead;
> Wisdom hides from them her treasure,
> Virtue bids them evil-speed!

> "Vainly may their hears, repenting,
> Seek for aid in future years;

Wisdom scorned knows no relenting;
Virtue is not won by tears.

"Fain would we your steps reclaim,
Waken fear and holy shame.
And to this end, our council well
And kindly doomed you to a cell
Whose darkness may, perchance, disclose
A beacon-guide from sterner woes."

So spake my judge — then seized his lamp
And left me in the dungeon damp,
A vault-like place whose stagnant air
Suggests and nourishes despair!

Rosina, this had never been
Except for you, my despot queen!
Except for you the billowy sea
Would now be tossing under me,
The wind's wild voice my bosom thrill
And my glad heart bound wilder still,
Flying before the rapid gale,
Those wondrous southern isles to hail
Which wait for my companions free
But thank your passion — not for me!

You know too well — and so do I —
Your haughty beauty's sovereignty;
Yet have I read those falcon eyes —
Have dived into their mysteries —
Have studied long their glance and feel
It is not love those eyes reveal.

They Flash, they burn with lightening shine,
But not with such fond fire as mine;
The tender star fades faint and wan

Before Ambition's scorching sun.
So deem I now — and Time will prove
If I have wronged Rosina's love.

"'Listen! When your hair, like mine'" is another Gondal dungeon poem; it too bears a title, "From a Dungeon Wall in the Southern College." The title here hints at a possible clue about the speaker's incarceration: it mentions a college, apparently some kind of severe learning institution, possibly part of the "Palace of Instruction," a Gondal place to which Brontë made reference in one of her short diary papers. The prisoner blames a woman, Rosina, who has played some part in his capture and for whom he feels a detrimental and powerful attraction, which is not requited. Based on the speech of the judge who tosses him into the dungeon, the captive has committed crimes against Stoicism: he has been lured by beauty, mirth, and earthly pleasure in derogation of duty and virtue. Presumably, given that this a Gondal poem, it advanced the Gondal narrative; however, it seems that the poem is more, or equally, concerned with pursuing the theme that living a life devoted to pleasure and mirth leads to unhappiness. John Keats expresses the same idea in "Ode on Melancholy": "Ay, in the very temple of delight / Veil'd Melancholy has her sovran shrine, / Though seen of none, save him whose strenuous tongue / Can burst Joy's grape against his palate fine; / His soul shall taste the sadness of her might, / And be among her cloudy trophies hung."

A little while, a little while,
The noisy crowd are barred away;
And I can sing and I can smile
A little while I've holyday!

Where wilt thou go, my harassed heart?
Full many a land invites thee now;
And places near and far apart
Have rest for thee, my weary brow.

There is a spot 'mid barren hills
Where winter howls and driving rain,
But if the dreary tempest chills
There is a light that warms again.

The house is old, the trees are bare
Moonless above bends twilight's dome
But what on earth is half so dear,
So longed for as the hearth of home?

The mute bird sitting on the stone,
The dank moss dripping from the wall,
The garden walk with weeds o'ergrown,
I love them — how I love them all!

Shall I go there? or shall I seek
Anther clime, another sky,
Where tongues familiar music speak
In accents dear to memory?

Yes, as I mused, the naked room,
The flickering firelight died away
And from the midst of cheerless gloom
I passed to bright, unclouded day —

A little and a lone green lane
That opened on a common wide;
A distant, dreamy, dim blue chain
Of mountains circling every side;

A heaven so clear, an earth so calm,
So sweet, so soft, so hushed an air
And, deepening still the dream-like charm,
Wild moor-sheep feeding everywhere —

That was the scene; I knew it well,
I knew the path-ways far and near
That winding o'er each billowy swell
Marked out the tracks of wandering deer.

Could I have lingered but an hour
It well had paid a week of toil,
But truth has banished fancy's power;
I hear my dungeon bars recoil —

Even as I stood with raptured eye
Absorbed in bliss so deep and dear
My hour of rest had fleeted by
And given me back to weary care.

"A little while, a little while" must be an expression of Emily
Brontë's own sentiments and experience, since she loathed living
away from home and preferred her solitude. She never lasted more
than two months in any boarding school situation as teacher or
student, except the Pensionnat Heger in Brussels, which she
attended with Charlotte. She stayed there for several months and
had agreed to a year. Emily and Charlotte went home before
planned because of the death of their aunt. Emily did not return
to finish the year, so Charlotte, intrepidly, made the journey back
by herself. Despite her not returning, Emily must have been deter-
mined at the outset to fight homesickness to achieve the goal of
learning French well enough to teach it at the boarding school that
the three sisters wanted to establish. Charlotte, Emily, and Anne
planned converting the parsonage into a school for a small number
of girls, thus earning a living and warding off the prospect of
working as governesses. As it turns out, no one responded to the
advertisements for the school, and the plan was abandoned.

In this poem the crowd and toil constitute confinement, and
freedom is gained for a brief time through thinking about places,
whether imaginary or real, such as home and beloved scenes in
nature. Once the brief respite comes to a close, the "dungeon bars"

rebound. In addition to the typical visualization of longed for places, this poem presents aural impressions to describe the difference between confinement and freedom. In captivity, the crowd is "noisy," and when the speaker must return, she does not see her bars recoil, she hears them. Much of the beauty of the imagined places resides in their sounds, or contrasting lack of sound: the bird on the wall is "mute"; there are the tones of the voices dear to memory; the natural spots are calm and hushed. Last, this poem furnishes an example of how lines lifted from Brontë's poems make ideal poetic aphorisms worthy to be embroidered: ". . . what on earth is half so dear, / So longed for as the hearth of home."

His land may burst the galling chain,
His people may be free again,
For them a thousand hopes remain,
But hope is dead for him.
Soft falls the moonlight on the sea
Whose wild waves play at liberty,
And Gondal's wind sings solemnly
Its native midnight hymn.

Around his prison walls it sings,
His heart is stirred through all its strings,
Because that sound remembrance brings
Of scenes that once have been.
His soul has left the storm below,
And reached a realm of sunless snow,
The region of unchanging woe,
Made voiceless by despair.

And Gerald's land may burst its chain,
His subjects may be free again;
For them a thousand hopes remain,
But hope is dead for him.
Set is his sun of liberty;
Fixed is his earthly destiny;

A few years of captivity,
And then a captive's tomb.

"His land may burst the galling chain" features a captured fighter named Gerald, a Gondal character, who apparently fought for his country's freedom but is now consigned to a dungeon for life. Although the poem for the most part tells of literal captivity, death imagery, suggesting that the dungeon represents death, permeates the last four lines of the second stanza: his soul inhabits the realm below, a land without sun and without change. Whether read as depicting a literal or metaphorical confinement, this poem implicates the topics mutability, death, and hope and despair in the following respects. Music in this poem summons images of the past, which parallels the effect of music in the "Mutability" poems. Here, the familiar hymn adds to the poignancy of the captive's suffering by evoking memories and striking at his heart. The presentation of death in this poem also adds to the various perspectives of death presented in poems that address death predominately and that appear in the chapter "Death." This captive does not view death as freedom or as the first step toward blissful eternity, but rather as continued imprisonment — when he dies he will be consigned to a captive's tomb. Without a single consoling or redemptive thought, this is admittedly a dark tale told darkly. Last, this poem could join the poems on despair in the chapter "Hope and Despair," since it pictures an implacable and endless situation. Regarding the causes of despair, Brontë's poems depict two: hopelessness for freedom, as shown in this poem, and grief. Both are states that are or seem unending, a crucial ingredient of despair.

CHAPTER SEVEN

Hope and Despair

In Emily Brontë's poetic world there are two contexts for considering hope and its nemesis, despair. First, is there reason to hope for a better life on earth or for some better state in the afterlife? In the group of poems addressing hope for a change in an individual's lot in life, at times Brontë denies the viability of hope because despair wields an indomitable power. In other poems, she carves out some reason not to despair and allows for some modest measure of hope for a change in one's daily existence. However, despair again triumphs if grief is at issue. Other poems turn away from even considering an improvement in life and set their sights on hope for an afterlife. That kind of hope enjoys a greater affirmation than hope for earthly existence, which does make sense: life has been experienced and found lacking, but what waits after death remains unknown and therefore is amenable to conjecture and, most importantly in Brontë's case, imagination. The challenge of topical categorization arises in placing her poems that address hope for a blissful eternity. Some of them predominately present themes relating to the topics of hope and despair. However, other closely related poems seem more expressive of ideas related to imagination or spirituality and join kindred poems in the chapters "Imagination" and "Spirituality."

Second, aside from the possibility that an individual has reason to hope for this life or the afterlife, certain poems address whether there is hope for an improvement in humankind in general. In that case, the conclusion is more unified and negative, as the poems on the whole consider Man devoid of virtue and life "a labor void and brief." The variety of treatment of the subject of hope and despair, and the differing conclusions, resemble her treatment of death, a topic on which she also takes several perspectives.

The recurring expressions in Brontë's poetry of near hopelessness or despair, either for the individual or humankind in general, make a strong statement, forcing one to wonder if Emily Brontë was not a sanguine person. Biographical evidence offers some clues as to whether we could justly read these statements as reflecting her own mind. On the one hand, she does not seem to have been negative or malcontent. She loved her home, including her family members and servants, and the moors. She had her compatriot in Anne in creating the Gondal saga. The two extant diary papers that she wrote bear no suggestion that she felt anything but an intense interest in Gondal and the tacit expectation of being around for at least three years from the date she wrote them. On the other hand, as a genius, she was a sort of separate species and felt ill at ease in the normal world. Certainly her life had its sorrows and tribulations. She had lost her mother and two sisters; death was a fixture in her life and thoughts; and her brother was a hopeless alcoholic causing endless difficulties and sadness, particularly for Mr. Brontë, who tried to control his son's lunatic ravings. Her attempts to earn a living — from publishing the volume of poetry, running a school, and writing a novel — failed. The inevitable prospect of losing her father and, upon his death, her income and home must have weighed upon her, as being a governess, the only recourse, was not something that she could have begun to tolerate. The poems offering a dispirited view of life as well as hope for eternity present a cohesiveness of thought and a direct and personal tone that identify those poems as expressions of her own mind. I would conclude, then, that Brontë did have a grim view of life, but equally possessed a self-created hopeful sense of something more than earthly existence.

Hope was but a timid friend;
She sat without my grated den,
Watching how my fate would tend,
Even as selfish-hearted men.

She was cruel in her fear;
Through the bars, one dreary day,
I looked out to see her there,
And she turned her face away!

Like a false guard, false watch keeping,
Still, in strife, she whispered peace;
She would sing while I was weeping;
When I listened, she would cease.

False she was, and unrelenting;
When my last joys strewed the ground,
Even Sorrow saw, repenting,
Those sad relics scattered round;

Hope — whose whisper would have given
Balm to all that frenzied pain —
Stretched her wings and soared to heaven;
Went — and ne'er returned again!

"Hope was but a timid friend" is surely one of Brontë's most thematically accessible poems. For one, it has a title, "Hope," and secondly it presents a sustained and clear personification of the idea of hope. Hope is a capricious, teasing, and unsympathetic creature who is even cruel because she actually has the ability as a heavenly creature to console, but refuses and finally leaves altogether. In the absence of hope comes despair, so this poem must weigh in on the side of hopelessness with regard to an individual achieving joy and peace in life.

Alone I sat; the summer day
Had died in smiling light away;
I saw it die, I watched it fade
From misty hill and breezeless glade;

And thoughts in my soul were gushing,
And my heart bowed beneath their power;
And tears within my eyes were rushing
Because I could not speak the feeling,
The solemn joy around me stealing
In that divine, untroubled hour.

I asked myself, "O why has heaven
Denied the precious gift to me,
The glorious gift to many given
To speak their thoughts in poetry?

"Dreams have encircled me," I said,
"From careless childhood's sunny time;
Visions by ardent fancy fed
Since life was in its morning prime."

But now, when I had hoped to sing,
My fingers strike a tuneless string;
And still the burden of the strain
Is "Strive no more; 'tis all in vain."

"Alone I sat; the summer day" stands out as unique in Brontë's
poetry as an autobiographical statement of her frustrations in
writing poetry — at least it would seem to be about herself. She
might have been imagining a poet who has lost his or her ability
to create, but since she is a poet, hearing her own voice in the poem
is ineluctable. In any event, the poem features a type of despair,
that of a writer who is equated with a musician who cannot strike
a tune, but must hear the repeated refrain advising him or her to
give it up as hopeless. Writing a poem to say that you cannot write
poetry imbues the poem with irony that nonetheless does not feel
intended.

In dungeons dark I cannot sing,
In sorrow's thrall 'tis hard to smile:

What bird can soar with broken wing?
What heart can bleed and joy the while?

"In dungeons dark I cannot sing" offers a brief justification for
feeling despair — it just cannot be helped in certain circumstances.
The state of despair is presented metaphorically as the inability to
sing in a dungeon, to smile while grieving, or to fly with a broken
wing. The dungeon motif, so familiar from the chapter "Captivity
and Freedom," has reappeared to serve as an illustration of a hope-
less situation. This is a Gondal poem, but, as I have noted, and is
certainly the case here, the Gondal designation has no bearing on
our reading of the poem and appreciating its thematic expression.

I know not how it falls on me,
This summer evening, hushed and lone;
Yet the faint wind comes soothingly
With something of an olden tone.

Forgive me if I've shunned so long
Your gentle greeting, earth and air!
But sorrow withers even the strong,
And who can fight against despair?

"I know not how it falls on me," like the previous poem and
many others, depicts despair as resulting from grief and as insur-
mountable. Addressing the wind, as in this poem, is a motif that
recurs very importantly in the poems in the chapters
"Imagination" and "Spirituality." The wind has been able in the
past to bring some comfort and now appears like an old friend;
however, in the present situation despair trumps the consoling
power of nature.

I'll not weep that thou art going to leave me,
There's nothing lovely here;
And doubly will the dark world grieve me
While thy heart suffers there.

I'll not weep, because the summer's glory
Must always end in gloom;
And, follow out the happiest story —
It closes with the tomb!

And I am weary of the anguish
Increasing winters bear:
I'm sick to see the spirit languish
Through years of dead despair.

So, if a tear, when thou art dying,
Should haply fall from me,
It is but that my soul is sighing
To go and rest with thee.

"I'll not weep that thou art going to leave me" presents an intractable despair: the world is devoid of charm in every way, the inevitability of death overwhelms life, and anguish from untold suffering, represented by "winter," all coalesce in a desire to quit life, such that the only reason to cry at the death of a loved one is in being left to live. As stated in the previous chapter "Captivity and Freedom," two conditions lead to despair in Brontë's poetic world: endless captivity and grief. This poem might seem to contradict that observation, as neither situation explicitly pertains, as here the reason for such despondency remains unprofessed, except for the lines about the inevitability of death. However, given the context of the poem, this might actually present another example of grief causing despair — anticipatory grief. The poem takes place as someone is about to die and leave the speaker to his or her grief.

May flowers are opening
And leaves unfolding free;
There are bees in every blossom
And birds on every tree.

The sun is gladly shining,
The stream sings merrily,
And I only am pining
And all is dark to me.

O cold, cold is my heart!
It will not cannot rise;
It feels no sympathy
With those refulgent skies.

Dead, dead is my joy,
I long to be at rest;
I wish the camp earth covered
This desolate breast.

If I were quite alone,
It might not be so drear,
When all hope was gone;
At least I could not fear.

But the glad eyes around me
Must weep as mine have done,
And I must see the same gloom
Eclipse their morning sun.

If heaven would rain on me
That future storm of care,
So their fond hearts were free
I'd be content to bear.

Alas! as lightning withers
The young and agèd tree,
Both they and I shall fall beneath
The fate we cannot flee.

"May flowers are opening" also gives despair the upper hand. Because of the deaths of loved ones, the speaker feels unable to appreciate the great beauty of nature and all joy is completely banished from her life. The greatest cause of despair, in this poem, is knowing that loved ones must inevitably grieve. That idea of enduring the sorrows of others as the worst kind of torment also appears in the poem "I know tonight the wind is sighing" in the chapter "Captivity and Freedom."

There should be no despair for you
While nightly stars are burning,
While evening sheds its silent dew
Or sunshine gilds the morning.

There should be no despair, though tears
May flow down like a river:
Are not the best beloved of years
Around your heart forever?

They weep — you weep — it must be so;
Winds sigh as you are sighing;
And Winter pours its grief in snow
Where Autumn's leaves are lying.

Yet they revive, and from their fate
Your fate cannot be parted,
Then journey onward, not elate,
But *never* brokenhearted.

"There should be no despair for you" veers slightly from the message that grief means despair and despair resists all solace. This poem offers the consoling notion that grief is shared by all as an undeniable part of life. That sentiment sounds like nothing more than the old adage "misery loves company"; however, psychology and philosophy embrace the notion that realizing the commonality and inescapabilty of suffering can serve as solace. This poem further points out that nature offers consolation in two ways: the beauty of nature should lift the spirit and the example of nature, with its pattern of renewal, suggests the same process in human life. Last, memories are another reason not to fall into despair; that strikes me as a rather non-Brontëan consolation because typically memories are more a source of pain than joy. Despite the encouragement not to despair, this poem offers only a moderate denial of despair and admits the impossibility of joy.

> **Month after month, year after year,**
> My harp has poured a dreary strain;
> At length a livelier note shall cheer,
> And pleasure tune its chords again.
>
> What though the stars and fair moonlight
> Are quenched in morning dull and grey?
> They are but tokens of the night,
> And *this*, my soul, is day.

"Month after month, year after year" uses the recurring motif of music to compare a state of sadness to a dreary tune. Hope imbues this poem through the image of the harp that will strike a more cheerful tone. Also, replacing the lost tokens of the night with what day can bring represents hope for something better in life.

> **What use is it to slumber here,**
> Though the heart be sad and weary?
> What use is it to slumber here,
> Though the day rise dark and dreary?
>
> For that mist may break when the sun is high,
> And this soul forget its sorrow;
> And the rosy ray of the closing day
> May promise a brighter morrow.

"What use to slumber here" could join the poems in the chapter "Death" that debate "to be or not to be"; however, its strong statement of hope places it here. The question is posed, why continue to "slumber here," i.e. continue to exist. The word "slumber" indicates that the speaker is so prostrate that his life has devolved into a semi-sleep state. The answer is hope; although there is no certainty of an improvement there is the possibility — the following day may bring something brighter, something less sorrowful.

Far away is the land of rest,
Thousand miles are stretched between,
Many a mountain's stormy crest,
Many a desert void of green.

Wasted, worn is the traveller;
Dark his heart and dim his eye;
Without hope or comforter,
Faultering, faint, and ready to die.

Often he looks to the ruthless sky,
Often he looks o'er his dreary road,
Often he wishes down to lie
And render up life's tiresome load.

But yet faint not, mournful man;
Leagues on leagues are left behind
Since your sunless course began;
Then go on to toil resigned.

If you still despair control,
Hush its whispers in your breast,
You shall reach the final goal,
You shall win the land of rest.

"Far away is the land of rest" uses the metaphor of a traveler to represent any person who plods through life beset by troubles and sorrow to the point of despair. Here, the narrator advises resignation to carry on, bolstered by the reality that life and its toil will not go on forever, since death will bring rest. There is no basis to hope for a better life, but the thought of death puts matters into perspective; thus, with the meager assurance that there is an end, the world-weary can carry-on. Death as rest is a common strain in Brontë's poetry, as it is in *Wuthering Heights* where Lockwood imagines Catherine, Edgar, and Heathcliff as sleepers in the quiet earth. An afterlife of rest promises the end of suffering, but falls far short of the more consoling notion of a blissful eternity in other poems, which appear particularly in the chapters "Imagination" and "Spirituality."

Fair sinks the summer evening now
In softened glory round my home;
The sky upon its holy brow
Wears not a cloud that speaks of gloom.

The old tower, shrined in golden light,
Looks down on the descending sun —
So gently evening blends with night,
You scarce can say that day is done.

And this is just the joyous hour
When we were wont to burst away,
To 'scape from labour's tyrant power
And cheerfully go out to play.

Then why is all so sad and lone?
No merry foot-step on the stair —
No laugh — no heart-awakening tone,
But voiceless silence everywhere.

I've wandered round our garden-ground,
And still it seemed, at every turn,
That I should greet approaching feet,
And words upon the breezes borne.

In vain — they will not come to-day,
And morning's beam will rise as drear;
Then tell me — are they gone for aye
Our sun blinks through the mists of care?

Ah no; reproving Hope doth say,
Departed joys 'tis fond to mourn,
When every storm that hides their ray
Prepares a more divine return.

"Fair sinks the summer evening now," like the preceding poem,
presents hope not for a change in one's daily life on earth but for
something better after death. More than mere rest from the toil of
life, this poem suggests a reunion with the divine. With that kind
of hope in hand, the grieving can turn sorrow to joy. The words
are spoken by a first person narrator who poses the question
whether the dead are really gone for good and who reports what
Hope replies.

Unlike many other poems, there are no quotation marks indi-
cating that Hope's answer comes from another voice, so apparently
the speaker figures out the solution for herself. Like the poem
immediately above, this poem fits very well with the poems on
grief in the chapter "Death." It continues the question posed in the
poem "'The winter wind is loud and wild'": why grieve for the
departed if they are in a better place. Also on the topic of death,
this poem, like "The busy day has hurried by," gives an immediate
visual and aural image of the actions and sensations of the bereft
with the lines: "I've wandered round our garden-ground, / And
still it seemed, at every turn, / That I should greet approaching
feet, and words upon the breezes borne." These two poems illus-
trate a technique that Brontë uses to great effect of evoking

emotions by situating them in the most common places: a hallway, a stairway, and a garden.

There was a time when my cheek burned
To give such scornful fiends the lie;
Ungoverned nature madly spurned
The law that bade it not defy.
O in the days of ardent youth
I would have given my life for truth.

For truth, for right, for liberty,
I would have gladly, freely died;
And now I calmly hear and see
The vain man smile, the fool deride;
Though not because my heart is tame,
Though not for fear, though not for shame.

My soul still chafes at every tone
Of selfish and self-blinded error;
My breast still braves the world alone,
Steeled as it ever was to terror;
Only I know, however I frown,
The same world will go rolling on.

"There was a time when my cheek burned" addresses hope for an improvement in mankind in general, rather than one's individual lot in life. The speaker is clearly jaded and defeated. This poem takes up the question whether humans are hopelessly flawed or amenable to improvement, entering the debate in the late 18th century and into the early 19th about the perfectibility of Man. Mary Shelley's father, William Godwin, was a famous advocate of the perfectibility of Man. We even find in the letters of John Keats that his acquaintances were still discussing that philosophical question; he described an acquaintance as a "Godwin-perfectibility man." Brontë, in this poem and others, finds no reason to hope for Man's improvement.

I am the only being whose doom
No tongue would ask, no eye would mourn;
I never caused a thought of gloom;
A smile of joy, since I was born.

In secret pleasure, secret tears,
This changeful life has slipped away,
As friendless after eighteen years,
As lone as on my natal day.

There have been times I cannot hide,
There have been times when this was drear,
When my sad soul forgot its pride
And longed for one to love me here.

But those were in the early glow
Of feelings since subdued by care;
And they have died so long ago,
I hardly now believe they were.

First melted of the hope of youth,
Then fancy's rainbow fast withdrew;
And then experience told me truth
In mortal bosoms never grew.

'Twas grief enough to think mankind
All hollow, servile, insincere;
But worse to trust to my own mind
And find the same corruption there.

"I am the only being whose doom" blends despair for a change
in one's own existence and for an improvement in Mankind. As for
the former, the speaker has given up hope of happiness. Added to
personal disappointments is her perception of the world at large
— all hollow, servile, and insincere. Indeed it appears that part of
the speaker's personal despair arises from the unvirtuous character

of the world, which has been pervasive enough to subvert her own mind. I have not considered chronology in my thematic analysis; however, given that the speaker mentions the passage of eighteen years and that there is a date on the poem, it is hard to resist checking whether the friendless eighteen years might correspond to her age. She was nineteen at the date of this poem. Aside from the personal and perhaps biographical expression of despair, there is an equally strong and negative one for mankind; however, the most trenchant statement about humanity is in the poem "How clear she shines! How quietly." Although that poem appears in the next chapter, the statement of despair for earthly existence bears quoting here to round out Brontë's depiction of the hopeless state of things in the world:

> Where, writhing 'neath the strokes of Fate,
> The mangled wretch was forced to smile;
> To match his patience 'gainst her hate,
> His heart rebellious all the while;
>
> Where Pleasure still will lead to wrong,
> And helpless Reason warn in vain;
> And Truth is weak, and Treachery strong;
> And Joy the surest path to Pain;
>
> And Peace, the lethargy of grief;
> And Hope, a phantom of the soul;
> And Life, a labour, void and brief;
> And Death, the despot of the whole!

CHAPTER EIGHT

Imagination

Emily Brontë wrote a poem on imagination which is very helpfully entitled "To Imagination." That poem so clearly treats the subject of imagination that it can serve as a touchstone to identify other poems, untitled and more abstruse of theme, as addressing the same subject. Even though imagination does not constitute a typical poetic subject, like nature, love, or death, Brontë wrote several poems that express themes similar to the main idea in "On Imagination" or that develop the same line of thought. What did imagination mean for Brontë, and why did she versify on that subject? I will answer those questions through recourse to her poems themselves, after some background information.

Imagination typically means the source of creativity in the arts. Of course that definition pertains to Brontë, who mined her imagination for characters, scenes, and story lines for Gondal, *Wuthering Heights*, and her poetry; however, that is not the sense of the word in this context. Here, imagination means the mind applied to one's own life — in Brontë's case, put to use to create her own inner world. Other writers have shared that understanding of imagination. John Milton expressed in *Paradise Lost* the notion that the internal world of the mind can compensate for or even replace externalities. When Satan takes stock of his deplorable situation, ousted from heaven and adrift on a burning lake, he concludes, so what, "The mind is its own place, and in itself / Can make a Heav'n of Hell, a Hell of Heav'n." John Keats echoed that expression in a letter, "The soul is a world of itself, and has enough to do in its own home." He further considered imagination unfettered by reality: "I feel more and more every day, as my imagination strengthens, that I do not live in this world alone but in a thousand worlds." He also described his imagination as a place apart from the world — a monastery — and he was its monk.

Brontë's reasons and aptitude for turning within and imagining her own world combine Satan and Keats. Just as Satan turned to his own mind to make a heaven of hell, Brontë sought refuge in her own world to escape reality, which she depicts as unfulfilling, grim, and hopeless in several poems, such as in the poem "When weary with the long day's care" in which she states, "So hopeless is the world without, / the world within I doubly prize." Again, in "I am the only being whose doom" in the chapter "Hope and Despair," she reveals disdain for the world, finding mankind "All hollow, servile, insincere." And she gives her manifesto on the state of life and earthly existence in the last four stanzas of the poem in this chapter, "How clear she shines, how quietly." Second, like Keats, Brontë was not chained to the real world, but could imagine others, and she could wander around alone but not lonely in her own mental sanctuary. Therefore, for Brontë, invoking the powers of imagination served the real and distinct purposes of finding tranquility in a troubled existence, escaping from the sordid and dreary, and overcoming fear of the unknown. And, her innate creativity made the escape to other worlds possible. Even understanding the uses of imagination, one might wonder why she wrote poems about it. Again, looking at her poems for clues, we see that her poems were vehicles in which she explored and developed the relationship with her imagination. Indeed, there is a progression in the development of imagination in the poems that begins with learning and ends with the defeat of death.

Although in other chapters I deduce Brontë's attitude and sentiments, from these poems I extract directly and unreservedly biographical information. I take them as Brontë's personal and authentic expressions of her own views rather than the analysis of a topic or the exercise of negative capability. These poems reveal above all that Brontë's relationship with her imagination surpassed the ordinary; it even went beyond what most could conceive of. Further we learn that, as the warden of her own sanctuary, Brontë would naturally prize solitude and disdain reality, confirming and explaining those two personality traits. The general impression that life was grim at the parsonage because it was remote and saw few visitors overlooks that Emily Brontë would not have wanted it any other way. Charlotte had wanderlust, but Emily did not because she roamed in her imagination. The poems on imagination have a particular power and memorable quality, which the authenticity of expression must underlie and explain.

A fine line distinguishes these poems and those placed in the chapter "Spirituality." Here, imagination creates visions of worlds beyond earthly, mortal existence; that world also includes a posthumous one, stepping into the realm of spirituality. However, these poems do not suggest that something else really does appear in the material world, separate from her own mind, whereas the poems in the chapter "Spirituality" (or some of them) do veer in that direction to envision a separate spirit-entity.

All day I've toiled, but not with pain,
In learning's golden mine;
And now at eventide again
The moonbeams softly shine.

There is no snow upon the ground,
No frost on wind or wave;
The south wind blew with gentlest sound
And broke their icy grave.

'Tis sweet to wander here at night
To watch the winter die,
With heart as summer sunshine light
And warm as summer sky.

O may I never lose the peace
That lulls me gently now,
Though time should change my youthful face,
And years should shade my brow!

True to myself, and true to all,
May I be healthful still,
And turn away from passion's call
And curb my own wild will.

"All day I've toiled, but not with pain" depicts the perfect state of tranquility: the speaker feels warm even in winter, at peace, and in a frame of mind that she would want to continue for her lifetime. The poem does not credit imagination for this state of happiness, but rather an extended and focused session of study. However, the time spent learning is closely related to indulging imagination. First, the effect described in this poem and that resulting from imagination are the same — a state of happiness and calm. Second, both studying and invoking one's imagination are solitary pursuits.

The poem emphasizes just how solitary her learning is by referring to having spent time in a "mine," suggesting a place removed and isolated from the world. In both cases, contentment results from the speaker's own inner experiences and not from any external event. Therefore, we can see this poem as presaging or complementing the poems that describe the powers of imagination *per se*. And, there is a last possible link: learning fuels imagination.

That wind, I used to hear it swelling
With joy divinely deep;
You might have seen my hot tears welling,
But rapture made me weep.

I used to love on winter nights
To lie and dream alone
Of all the rare and real delights
My early years had known;

And oh, above the rest of those
That coming time should bear,

Like heaven's own glorious stars they rose
Still beaming bright and fair.

"That wind I used to hear it swelling" introduces the wind,
which will play various yet similar roles in these poems; here, it
brings a sensation of joy and evokes thoughts of early years. In
other poems, it lures the speaker in the poem away from reality,
such as in "Shall Earth no more inspire thee," which appears in
the chapter "Nature." At its most effective, the wind unleashes
the speaker's imagination and transports her to other worlds. I
know of no literary precedent that Brontë could have read to
inspire such a relationship with the wind. She obviously lived in
a particularly windy clime, as anyone knows who remembers
Lockwood's explanation of the word "wuthering" in the novel
Wuthering Heights. However, that does not explain the unique
power of the wind and breeze in Brontë's poetic world to trigger
her powers of imagination. Accepting the impossibility of
explaining such a personal phenomenon, we can nonetheless see
the result, such as in this poem. The wind brings thoughts of the
past, some of which are simply imaginary more than remem-
brance because they are not "real delights," but rare and
dreamlike.

Moving on from considerations of natural forces and the set-
ting of the poem, to the narration, a question arises: who is "you"
in the third line of the second stanza? The speaker might be
addressing the wind, but an address to the wind in the second
person does not fit with the first line, which makes reference to
"that wind." There seems to be some other observer.

I'm happiest when most away
I can bear my soul from its home of clay
On a windy night when the moon is bright
And the eye can wander through worlds of light —

When I am not and none beside —
Nor earth nor sea nor cloudless sky —

But only spirit wandering wide
Through infinite immensity.

"I'm happiest when most away" establishes that an internal power, i.e. imagination, transports the speaker away from the "home of clay" i.e. earthly existence. She precisely says "*I* can bear my soul" (emphasis added). The effect differs from the two preceding poems because she escapes and achieves happiness in her own world rather than gaining peace or contentment in this world. The catalyst for the exercise of her inner power is the wind, again, joined by the moon and the night sky. The liberating power of the night reminds us of the poem "Ah! Why because the dazzling sun," in the chapter "Nature." There, the night sky enthralls the speaker of the poem, whereas sunlight and day obtrude harshly and destructively.

In summer's mellow midnight,
A cloudless moon shone through
Our open parlour window
And rosetrees wet with dew.

I sat in silent musing,
The soft wind waved my hair:
It told me Heaven was glorious,
And sleeping Earth was fair.

I needed not its breathing
To bring such thoughts to me,
But still it whispered lowly,
"How dark the woods will be!

"The thick leaves in my murmur
Are rustling like a dream,
And all their myriad voices
Instinct with spirit seem."

I said, "Go, gentle singer,
Thy wooing voice is kind,
But do not think its music
Has power to reach my mind.

"Play with the scented flower,
The young tree's supple bough,
And leave my human feelings
In their own course to flow."

The wanderer would not leave me;
Its kiss grew warmer still —
"O come," it sighed so sweetly,
"I'll win thee 'gainst they will.

"Have we not been from childhood friends?
Have I not loved thee long?
As long as thou hast loved the night
Whose silence wakes my song.

"And when thy heart is laid at rest
Beneath the church-yard stone
I shall have time enough to mourn
And thou to be alone."

"In summer's mellow midnight" personifies the wind as a dear, faithful, and influential friend. The poem is entitled "The Night Wind," so there is no doubt as to the subject. Like the poem above, the setting is a moonlit night, which "wakes" the wind's "song." There is a dialogue in this poem that establishes the long and meaningful relationship the speaker has enjoyed with the wind. The poem does not elaborate on the effect the wind will have if only the speaker in the poem succumbs to it, but the second stanza indicates that a sense of well-being on earth and glory in heaven will arise, a feeling which her imagination has conceived of already on its own, as she states: "I needed not its breathing / to bring such

thoughts to me." Although these poems like to depict the wind
unleashing imagination, that fiction reverses cause and effect for a
poetic result, as it takes imagination to impute such powers to an
atmospheric disturbance.

> **Aye, there it is! It wakes tonight**
> Sweet thoughts that will not die
> And feelings fires flash as bright
> As in the years gone by!
>
> And I can tell by thine altered cheek
> And by they kindled gaze
> And by the words thou scarce dost speak,
> How wildly fancy plays.
>
> Yes, I could swear that glorious wind
> Has swept the world aside,
> Has dashed its memory from thy mind
> Like foam-bells from the tide —
>
> And thou art now a spirit pouring
> Thy presence into all —
> The essence of the Tempest's roaring
> And of the Tempest's fall —
>
> A universal influence
> From Thine own influence free;
> A principle of life, intense,
> Lost to mortality.
>
> Thus truly when that breast is cold
> Thy prisoned soul shall rise,
> The dungeon mingle with the mould —
> The captive with the skies.

"Aye, there it is! It wakes tonight" makes even more explicit the effect of imagination set loose by the wind: the earthly world is swept away and the soul takes flight. That liberation also portends a similar experience after death, as imagination can likewise conjure a free and eternal state after death. The transformation from body to spirit in this poem is similar to what occurs in the poems more pointedly about spirituality. The differentiating factor, as noted at the end of the introductory discussion to the chapter, is that here imagination alone, and no outward cause, has liberated the soul. The curious thing about this poem is the second person narration. The speaker seems to be talking about herself, but uses the second person as if addressing someone else. She is standing outside of herself chronicling the effect of "fancy" (a synonym for imagination). At the end, the motif of captivity and freedom appears and echoes the poems discussed in the chapter "Captivity and Freedom" that present figurative dungeons. In this poem there is no question that death constitutes freedom for the captive of life. Motifs, like the dungeon, surface here and there in Brontë's poetry to blend and bind diverse poems and to put a signature on her work.

How clear she shines! How quietly
I lie beneath her silver light
While Heaven and Earth are whispering me,
"To morrow wake, but dream to-night."

Yes, Fancy, come, my Fairy love!
These throbbing temples, softly kiss;
And bend my lonely couch above
And bring me rest and bring me bliss.

The world is going — Dark world, adieu!
Grim world, go hide thee till the day;
The heart thou canst not all subdue
Must still resist if thou delay!

Thy love I will not, will not share;
Thy hatred only wakes a smile;
Thy griefs may wourid — thy wrongs may tear,
But, oh, thy lies shall ne'er beguile!

While gazing on the stars that glow
Above me in that stormless sea,
I long to hope that all the woe
Creation knows, is held in thee!

And this shall be my dream to-night —
I'll think the heaven of glorious spheres
Is rolling on its course of light
In endless bliss, through endless years;

I'll think there's not one world above,
Far as these straining eyes can see,
Where Wisdom ever laughed at Love,
Or Virtue crouched to Infamy;

Where, writhing 'neath the strokes of Fate,
The mangled wretch was forced to smile;
To match his patience 'gainst her hate,
His heart rebellious all the while;

Where Pleasure still will lead to wrong,
And helpless Reason warn in vain;
And Truth is weak and Treachery strong,
And Joy the surest path to Pain;

And Peace, the lethargy of grief;
And Hope, a phantom of the soul;
And Life, a labour, void and brief;
And Death, the despot of the whole!

"How clear she shines! How quietly" bears a title eponymous with the first sentence in the opening line. What is "she?" She is fancy, a synonym for imagination. The speaker calls to her imagination to bring rest and bliss by making the dark world go away. Unlike the previous poems, the wind does not free her mind, but nature still plays a part. Night and the moon form the backdrop; although the moon is not explicitly mentioned it is suggested by the silver light. That glow of silver light also belongs to imagination, such that the moon and imagination appear unified. The speaker also addresses the dark world, bidding it farewell and declaring that she need not have any part of it because she will imagine other worlds where its miserable attributes do not exist. This poem is exceptional not only in clearly showing that imagination provides an escape from the reality, but also in the spectacular last four stanzas that crescendo in a litany describing life in all its misery.

That manifesto reiterates her statement in another poem that the "word without" is hopeless — an idea that we have also seen in the poems addressing captivity and freedom and hope and despair. In the list of the final stanzas describing the ills of the world, Brontë discounts joy with the statement, "And Joy the shortest path to Pain." A similar sentiment appears in the poem "'Listen! When your hair like mine.'" There, the lines by the stern judge denigrate mirth as leading to disappointment. Those views of joy might remind one of John Keats's poem "Ode on Melancholy" and its central notion that the person who knows joy, who "Can burst Joy's grape against his palate fine," will end up a trophy of Sadness.

When weary with the long day's care,
And earthly change from pain to pain,
And lost, and ready to despair,
Thy kind voice calls me back again —
O, my true friend, I am not lone
While then canst speak with such a tone!

So hopeless is the world without,
The world within I doubly prize;
Thy world where guile and hate and doubt
And cold suspicion never rise;
Where thou and I and Liberty,
Have undisputed sovereignty.

What matters it that all around
Danger and grief and darkness lie,
If but within our bosom's bound
We hold a bright unsullied sky,
Warm with ten thousand mingled rays
Of suns that know no winter days?

Reason indeed may oft complain
For Nature's sad reality,
And tell the suffering heart how vain
Its cherished dreams must always be;
And Truth may rudely trample down
The flowers of Fancy newly blown.

But thou art ever there to bring
The hovering visions back and breathe
New glories o'er the blighted spring
And call a lovelier life from death,
And whisper with a voice divine
Of real worlds as bright as thine.

I trust not to thy phantom bliss,
Yet still in evening's quiet hour
With never-failing thankfulness
I welcome thee, benignant power,
Sure solacer of human cares
And brighter hope when hope despairs.

"When weary with the long day's care," is entitled "To

Imagination," and, as that title would suggest, the speaker
addresses Imagination in this poem, confiding her feelings to it;
the use of the word "thine," meaning "yours," is directed at
Imagination. Here the power of imagination confronts three
formidable forces: Reason, Nature, and Truth. Imagination
prevails, having the power to bring to mind the beauties of spring,
create memories of the departed better than those justified by life,
and give a glimpse of other worlds. As to the latter, it is only a
glimpse, as indicated by the word "whisper." How strong is her
imagination in the end, despite the marvels it has performed for
her? At the start she calls imagination her true friend, with a kind
voice, and in the second and third stanzas it is her steadfast compa-
triot; however, imagination does not yet merit complete trust,
having a phantom nature. As in the previous poem, imagination
provides escape from the world that is depicted without redeeming
feature, indeed it is hopeless. As noted in the immediately
preceding discussion, there is a connection here to those poems on
hope and despair that depict Mankind and his chances of improve-
ment as hopeless. The only solution is "the world within."

One curious aspect of the poem is that Nature, along with
Reason and Truth, stands opposed to Imagination and is associ-
ated with "sad reality." In numerous other instances Nature serves
Brontë as consolation for the shortcomings of existence; however,
here the role of nature is like that which appears in "Methinks this
heart should rest awhile," where the spectacle of winter is a *memento
mori*.

> O thy bright eyes must answer now,
> When Reason, with a scornful brow,
> Is mocking at my overthrow;
> O thy sweet tongue must plead for me
> And tell why I have chosen thee !
>
> Stern Reason is to judgment come
> Arrayed in all her forms of gloom:
> Wilt thou my advocate be dumb?

No, radiant angel, speak and say
Why I did cast the world away;

Why I have persevered to shun
The common paths that others run;
And on a strange road journeyed on
Heedless alike of Wealth and Power —
Of Glory's wreath and Pleasure's flower.

These, once, indeed, seemed Beings divine,
And they perchance heard vows of mine
And saw my offerings on their shrine —
But, careless gifts are seldom prized,
And mine were worthily despised;

So with a ready heart I swore
To seek their altar-stone no more,
And gave my spirit to adore
Thee, ever-present, phantom thing —
My slave, my comrade, and my King!

A slave, because I rule thee still;
Incline thee to my changeful will
And make thy influence good or ill —
A comrade, for by day and night
Thou art my intimate delight —

My Darling Pain that wounds and sears
And wrings a blessing out from tears
By deadening me to real cares;
And yet, a king — though prudence well
Have taught thy subject to rebel.

And am I wrong to worship where
Faith cannot doubt nor Hope despair
Since my own soul can grant my prayer?

Speak, God of Visions, plead for me
And tell why I have chosen thee!

"O thy bright eyes must answer now" analyzes the relationship between the poet and her imagination, showing levels of complexity. She addresses her imagination, referring to it as having "bright eyes," and calling it by various names: a radiant angel, phantom thing, my Darling Pain, God of Visions, and her slave, comrade, and king. Like the poem above, Imagination, offering escape from reality, confronts Reason, which is stern and gloomy. Further, and unlike the preceding poems, she recounts how at one time earthly concerns meant something to her before she turned away from the world without to the world within, to borrow her own expression. This poem also takes a further step in the progression of the power of imagination. First, there is a greater trust in the power of imagination than in the previous poem and no doubt as to its efficacy. Even though she still refers to it in one instance as a phantom thing, it is nonetheless "ever present." Yet, the poem bespeaks a near crisis, as if the speaker needs assurance, even though the benefits of the mindset that she has fashioned are enormous.

In her inner world there is no external force that can interfere. Faith cannot doubt and Hope cannot despair because she is entirely self-sufficient in creating her world: she, herself, her soul will grant her prayers. Second, this poem begins to equate imagination to religion and God. Words in the last stanza — "worship," "prayer," and "God" — strike a worshipful, even religious tone. We have seen imagination offer peace, escape from a dreary day and then from painful, worthless earthly existence, and now it is answering prayers. Her god is of her own creation, immune from all external forces; having never existed, it cannot be destroyed. That idea of indestructibility centers the next poem as well. The value of non-existence, in particular its beauty, is a strain that is heard in "Ode on a Grecian Urn," when John Keats declares that imagined things are better because they cannot end: "Heard melodies are sweet, but those unheard / are sweeter; therefore, ye soft pipes, play on; / Not to the sensual ear, but, more endear'd, / Pipe to the spirit ditties of no tone."

Turning to what one can imagine as the answer to confronting existence is not common and probably not possible for most. However, as discussed in introducing this chapter, that system does connect with ideas of other writers, John Milton and John Keats. Also, Brontë's idea, with its focus on self-sufficiency, has a distant relation in certain philosophies that counsel the relative unimportance of the external world — the opinions of others, notoriety, wealth — in favor of self-sufficiency and a state of tranquility obtained through one's own thoughts. Roman Stoicism, in particular, although starting at a point distant from Brontë's, winds up close to the same place. That comparison in no way suggests that Brontë read or was influenced by any philosophy in developing her use of imagination, but only notes the coincidence of ideas. John Keats described that phenomenon of similar thoughts from disparate individuals in a letter: "Minds would leave each other in contrary directions, traverse each other at numberless points, and at last greet each other at the journey's end."

No coward soul is mine
No trembler in the world's storm-troubled sphere
I see Heaven's glories shine
And Faith shines equal arming me from Fear

O God within my breast
Almighty ever-present Deity
Life, that in me hast rest,
As I Undying Life, have power in Thee

Vain are the thousand creeds
That move men's hearts, unutterably vain,
Worthless as withered weeds
Or idlest froth amid the boundless main

To waken doubt in one
Holding so fast by thy infinity
So surely anchored on
The steadfast rock of Immortality

With wide-embracing love
Thy spirit animates eternal years
Pervades and broods above,
Changes, sustains, dissolves, creates and rears

Though earth and moon were gone
And suns and universes ceased to be
And Thou wert left alone
Every Existence would exist in thee

There is not room for Death
Nor atom that his might could render void
Since thou art Being and Breath
And what thou art may never be destroyed.

"No coward Soul is mine" continues the development of an inner world through the power of imagination. The speaker refers in the second stanza to god as one with and the same as herself, just as she spoke of her own power to answer her own prayers in the poem above. She has progressed from calling her imagination "God of Visions" in the previous poem to the God within her breast in this poem, i.e. the god of her own creation, and she no longer admits any weakness. Because her god and her world are of her own creation "what thou art" is indestructible, just as she referred to her imaginary world as impervious to the external world and its deleterious forces because it does not have a real existence.

The word "faith" appears in the first stanza; that word has strong connotations to a belief in God. I do not think that Brontë intends that connotation. In her word hoard, "faith" means simply a belief in something. For example, in "Death that struck when I was most confiding," the speaker states that she has had a "certain Faith of

Joy to be," meaning that she believed that joy was possible. Likewise when Heathcliff declares that he has a "faith" in ghosts, he is simply saying he believes in ghosts. So here, faith standing equal to death refers to her belief (such as she has developed it herself), not faith in god in a Christian context. As mentioned before, imagination as presented in Brontë's poems grows in ever-increasing usefulness from facilitating a day dream, to escaping from a cruel existence, to creating an inner world, and such a world that includes a boundless eternity and that excludes death: "There is not room for Death / Nor atom that his might could render void."

CHAPTER NINE

Spirituality

A working definition of spirituality emerges from this group of poems: a sense of or belief in things, occurrences, or places that are not of the material world. Spirituality poems might pose some difficulties in comprehension because they express a sensation that is not real and, in Brontë's case, so intensely singular and personal that the common ground of shared experience is scarce or nonexistent. Ralph Waldo Emerson, who was akin to Brontë in his reverence for nature and in having a personal belief system, thought that expressing spirituality was a non-starter: "Of that ineffable essence, which we call Spirit, he that thinks most, will say least." That sounds like good advice for the conversationalist or essayist, but less applicable to the poet, who will find a worthy way to utter the feeling. Brontë devotes many lines to describing, first, how a sense of something beyond the real word arises: through nature, in a dream-like state, via imagination, and even from experience with life. Then, she delineates what the spiritual event is like: an actual vision; a suggestion of a vision; a glimmer, sound or feeling — all perceptions that would not appear to anyone else and that defy the material world. Last, there is the overall result of the experience: a sense of comfort, an understanding of how to confront life, or the certainty that earthly existence does not define the limit.

Strains from the poems on nature, mutability, death, hope and despair, and imagination resound in the poems on spirituality. Why do those five topics figure in poems about spirituality? Nature frequently galvanizes the spiritual experience; mutability is the state of things that makes spirituality necessary; death, like mutability, forces the mind toward spiritual beliefs to make sense of that inevitability; hope verbalizes the desire that beyond the tangible world there is another one free of life's vicissitudes; and imagination envisions states beyond the material world. With regard to the last in the list, poems on imagination and spirituality might prove mostly indistinguishable from each other. One distinction, however, reflected in two poems in this chapter, is the presence of an actual spirit — an entity, more than a personification, metaphor, or product of the mind.

Spiritual matters center several themes in *Wuthering Heights* and those statements add to an understanding of Brontë's view on spirituality. Heathcliff's character conveys themes on three spiritual topics: heaven, the soul, and ghosts. One notion in the novel is that heaven is a personal construct, such that one man's heaven might be another's hell. Heathcliff execrates the traditional heaven and believes he will attain his heaven that consists of some kind of afterlife with Catherine and nothing more. Second, his belief in the afterlife indicates that he also advocates the existence of a soul, since he must intend that his soul and Catherine's will join after death. Also, Brontë develops a theme about ghosts, which are another manifestation of the soul, through Heathcliff's actions and words. When Lockwood cries out that there is an apparition at the window, Heathcliff does not question that it is Catherine's ghost because he so desperately wants it to be. He further tells Nelly point blank that he believes in them and therefore stands a chance that Catherine will haunt him. Through those scenes and statements, Brontë depicts that the bereft grasp at notions that deny the finality of death. She does not proffer ghosts — the novel is not a gothic tale. She makes it clear that any sightings of apparitions occur under conditions where the credibility of the viewer is easily impeached.

In addition to Heathcliff's statements relating to spirituality, Nelly rhapsodizes to Lockwood about a glorious hereafter, advocating the more traditional notion of heaven and eternity, and Catherine foresees a posthumous state incomparably above and beyond worldly existence, which also blends the notions of freedom, rest, and a return to nature.

In parsing together Brontë's spiritual belief system, the notions expressed in *Wuthering Heights* would not necessarily be hers; however, when similar ideas surface in a poem, the reiteration suggests the importance to Brontë of those ideas. Therefore, the poems in this chapter add to an understanding of Brontë's own spiritual perspective, just as the poems on imagination reflect her own views, and the same reasons support both conclusions: the tone of directness and authenticity and the suitability of the beliefs to her manner of living argue in favor of those expressions as Brontë's own. Based on the treatment of spirituality in *Wuthering Heights* and in these self-expressive poems, one can conclude that Brontë believed that heaven is a personal construct, that the mind creates its own reality, and that death ushers in eternal rest, freedom, and even something blissful or rewarding. That blissful eternity either results simply because life's sufferings are over forever or because imagination has envisioned it. Although knowing the precise contours of her spiritual vision defies us, we can conclude that Brontë unquestionably took great comfort from it.

The night was dark, yet winter breathed
With softened sighs on Gondal's shore;
And, though its wind repining grieved,
It chained the snow-swollen streams no more.

How deep into the wilderness
My horse had strayed, I cannot say;
But neither morsel nor caress
Would urge him further on the way;

So, loosening from his neck the rein,
I set my worn companion free;
And billowy hill and boundless plain
Full soon divided him from me.

The sullen clouds lay all unbroken
And blackening round the horizon drear;

But still they gave no certain token
Of heavy rain or tempests near.

I paused, confounded and distressed;
Down in the heath my limbs I threw;
Yet wilder as I longed for rest
More wakeful heart and eyelids grew.

It was about the middle night,
And under such a starless dome
When, gliding from the mountain's height,
I saw a shadowy spirit come.

Her wavy hair, on her shoulders bare,
It shone like soft clouds round the moon;
Her noiseless feet, like melting sleet,
Gleamed white a moment, then were gone.

"What seek you now, on this bleak moor's brow?
Where wanders that form from heaven descending?"
It was thus I said as, her graceful head,
The spirit above my couch was bending.

"This is my home, where whirlwinds blow,
Where snowdrifts round my path are swelling;
'Tis many a year, 'tis long ago,
Since I beheld another dwelling.

"When thick and fast the smothering blast
O'erwhelmed the hunter on the plain,
If my cheek grew pale in its loudest gale
May I never tread the hills again.

"The shepherd had died on the mountainside,
But my ready aid was near him then:

I led him back o'er the hidden track
And gave him to his native glen.

"When tempests roar on the lonely shore,
I light my beacon with sea-weeds dry,
And it flings its fire through the darkness dire
And gladdens the sailor's hopeless eye.

"And the scattered sheep, I love to keep
Their timid forms to guard from harm;
I have a spell, and they know it well,
And I save them with a powerful charm.

"Thy own good steed on his friendless bed
A few hours since you left to die;
But I knelt by his side and the saddle untied,
And life returned to his glazing eye.

"And deem thou not that quite forgot
My mercy will forsake me now:
I bring thee care and not despair;
Abasement but not overthrow.

"To a silent home thy foot may come
And years may follow of toilsome pain;
But yet I swear by that burning tear
The loved shall meet on its hearth again."

"The night was dark, yet winter breathed" might come as a surprise at this juncture because it is a Gondal poem. Even though we are deep into Brontë's own powers of mind and beliefs, I include a Gondal poem (not that the one mention of Gondal matters much, if at all) because it presents a literal spirit apparition. That assertion comes with the caveat that most things can fit a metaphorical interpretation; indeed, there is no reason not to see the spirit in this poem as a kinder version of "Hope," who in

an earlier poem was a timid friend. More than because of its
Gondal designation, this poem stands out from this group of spir-
ituality poems because it sounds in tone more like a fairy tale than
a mystical experience, since this spirit is helping the sheep and
the horse with spells and charms. The lovely thirteenth stanza
sings like a nursery rhyme (a beautiful and sophisticated one) and
sticks like one too: "And the scattered sheep, I love to keep / their
timid forms to guard from harm; / I have a spell, and they know
it well, / and I save them with a powerful charm." Alternatively,
the spirit's arrival is amenable to being read as a dream, since the
narrator is exhausted and it is the middle of the night, such that
his own mind is answering his prayers. In support of the dream
theory, dreams figure largely in *Wuthering Heights*: Lockwood has
his two dreams when he is stranded at Wuthering Heights,
Catherine has a dream that she insists on telling Nelly although
Nelly resists because she is superstitious about dreams, and Nelly
has a dream about Heathcliff's death. Also in the poems under
"Mutability" the experience of reflecting on the past is often
described as a dream. Even taking the spirit as a fairy-like appari-
tion, the setting connects this poem to those presenting a more
identifiable extra-sensory experience. In those, as in this poem,
nature provides the background to the experience; here, we are
under the night sky, amidst the mountains.

And like myself lone, wholly lone,
It sees the day's long sunshine glow;
And like myself it makes its moan
In unexhausted woe.

Give we the hills our equal prayer;
Earth's breezy hills and heaven's blue sea;
We ask for nothing further here
But our own hearts and liberty.

Ah! Could my hand unlock its chain
How gladly would I watch it soar,

And ne'er regret and ne'er complain
To see its shining eyes no more.

But let me think that if to-day
It pines in cold captivity,
To-morrow both shall soar away,
Eternally, entirely Free.

"And like myself lone, wholly lone" presents a bifurcated iden-
tity. Who or what is "it" and who is the additional presence that
gives rise to the plural pronoun "we"? I favor the supposition that
"it" means her soul. First, the reference to unlocking its chain in
the third stanza hints that her soul is her other half because in the
following poem she refers to herself as having a "chainless soul."
Further, throughout the poem, "it" fits the notion of a soul because
of its unity with the speaker, as opposed to appearing as a separate
entity. Also, a soul might be considered the better part of a person,
and here, "it" is the more hopeful part of the amalgamation, having
"shining eyes." Should one prefer a material interpretation of this
poem, the "it" could be viewed as a bird in captivity. Lending some
support to the idea that Brontë either depicts a bird, or uses bird
imagery, is the fact that Brontë owned a bird, a hawk. In either
case, the "tomorrow," when both the speaker and the bird will be
free, does not literally signify the upcoming day, but rather would
seem to mean the arrival of death, echoing the motif of freedom
from captivity through dying from the metaphorical poems on
captivity discussed in the chapter "Captivity and Freedom."
However, the desire for "liberty" in the second stanza does not
seem like a desire for freedom through death. The same plea for
liberty appears in the next poem, and similarly a call for liberty
figures in the poem, "When weary with the long day's care," in the
chapter "Imagination." There, the speaker says to her imagination
that the ideal world will allow "thou, and I and Liberty . . . undis-
puted sovereignty." Liberty in all three poems conveys an
unfettered state while on earth, free of the woe and recklessness
that Brontë has identified as plaguing life in several poems.

Although the method for freedom is less clear in this poem, knowing the message from other poems leads to the conclusion that such an unfettered state will be achieved for herself and her soul through imagination.

> **Riches I hold in light esteem**
> And Love I laugh to scorn
> And lust of Fame was but a dream
> That vanished with the morn —
>
> And if I pray, the only prayer
> That moves my lips for me
> Is — "Leave the heart that now I bear
> And give me liberty."
>
> Yes, as my swift days near their goal
> 'Tis all that I implore —
> Through life and death, a chainless soul
> With courage to endure!

"Riches I hold in light esteem" echoes the immediately preceding poem in motif and diction, with a call for liberty and a "chainless soul." Here the separation of self from soul is absent, but there is another aspect of her identity: the heart, "the heart that now I bear," which she wants to leave behind. The heart seems to represent her corporeal self and her suffering inflicted by life. I have not in the topical approach of this book focused on when any poem was written; however, here I will point out that the immediately preceding poem and this one were written days apart, on February 27, 1841 and March 1, 1841, which is not surprising given their similarity. Biographically, assuming this is Brontë's own voice in this poem, it is strange that at the age of twenty-two she states "as my swift days near their goal," meaning that she was fast approaching death. She did not suffer from bad health until she contracted consumption years later, from which she died at the age of twenty-nine.

On a sunny brae alone I lay
One summer afternoon;
It was the marriage-time of May
With her young lover, June.

From her Mother's heart seemed loath to part
That queen of bridal charms,
But her Father smiled on the fairest child
He ever held in his arms.

The trees did wave their plumy crests,
The glad birds carolled clear;
And I, of all the wedding guests,
Was only sullen there.

There was not one, but wished to shun
My aspect void of cheer;
The very gray rocks, looking on,
Asked, "What do you here?"

And I could utter no reply:
In sooth, I did not know
Why I had brought a clouded eye
To greet the general glow.

So, resting on a heathy bank,
I took my heart to me;
And we together sadly sank
Into a reverie.

We thought, "When winter comes again,
Where will these bright things be?
All vanished, like a vision vain,
An unreal mockery!

"The birds that now so blithely sing,
Through deserts frozen dry,
Poor spectres of the perished Spring,
In famished troops will fly.

"And why should we be glad at all?
The leaf is hardly green,
Before a token of its fall
Is on the surface seen."

Now whether it were really so,
I never could be sure;
But as, in fit of peevish woe,
I stretched me on the moor,

A thousand thousand glancing fires
Seemed kindling in the air;
A thousand thousand silvery lyres
Resounded far and near:

Methought the very breath I breathed
Was full of sparks divine,
And all my heather-couch was wreathed
By that celestial shine.

And while the wide earth echoing rang
To that strange minstrelsy,
The little glittering spirits sang,
Or seemed to sing, to me:

"O mortal, mortal let them die;
Let Time and Tears destroy,
That we may overflow the sky
With universal joy.

"Let grief distract the sufferer's breast,
And night obscure his way;
They hasten him to endless rest,
And everlasting day.

"To thee the world is like a tomb,
A desert's naked shore;
To us, in unimagined bloom,
It brightens more and more.

"And, could we lift the veil, and give
One brief glimpse to thine eye
Thou wouldst rejoice for those that live,
Because they live to die."

The music ceased — the noonday Dream,
Like dream of night, withdrew
But Fancy, still, will sometimes deem
Her fond creation true.

"On a sunny brae alone I lay" continues several elements we have
seen before. One is the "heart" as a separate part of a person, as in
the immediately preceding poem. Also imagination reappears as
the source of a vision, identified as such at the end of the poem
when the speaker refers to what she has experienced as the
"creation" of "Fancy." The title, "A Daydream," supports the
notion that the apparition and singing are not reliable, but a kind
of dream, brought on by imagination. The statement about the
power of imagination in this poem resembles very closely the ideas
in the poems discussed in the chapter "Imagination"; however,
here the fantastical experience is more fully developed and celes-
tial: the air is full of sparks, there are lyres and strange singing, and
a disembodied voice speaks unambiguous words about the beauty
of death. Another notable feature distinguishes this poem from
those on imagination and paints it a decidedly spiritual hue: the
vision occurs during the day and not at night when the moon is

bright and the breeze is seductively blowing. Most importantly, the celestial voice arrives without any catalyst at all, like an entirely separate and real entity. In presenting such a defined visual and aural experience, this poem exceeds those already discussed as a mystical vision, yet it still lacks complete assurance: the speaker equivocates in the last stanza about the reality of her vision. Two other poems still to come, which envision states beyond reality and after death, evince greater certainty in the spiritual experience, with the introduction of a "comforter." They appear at the end of this chapter.

The example of the seasons and winter laying waste to summer's beauties, in the seventh stanza, must seem familiar to us now. The particular focus here on the eventual exodus of song birds from the plumy crests of the trees, bring to mind a similar image for winter's birdless trees in sonnet LXXIII by Shakespeare: "Bare ruin'd choirs where late the sweet birds sang." The reminder of death in nature, coupled with a general sadness, launch the reverie of the speaker, who is reclining on a slope. The discussion of a marriage in the first two stanzas represents the time of year, the beginning of June, and the trees and other natural things are present at the nuptials, i.e. are flourishing in the early summer landscape.

> **"Enough of Thought, Philosopher;**
> Too long hast thou been dreaming
> Unlightened, in this chamber drear
> While summer's sun is beaming —
> Space-sweeping soul, what sad refrain
> Concludes thy musings once again?
>
> *"Oh, for the time when I shall sleep*
> *Without identity,*
> *And never care how rain may steep*
> *Or snow may cover me!*
>
> *"No promised heaven, these wild Desires,*
> *Could all, or half fulfil;*

No threatened Hell, with quenchless fires,
Subdue this quenchless will!"

— So said I, and still say the same;
— Still, to my death, will say —
Three Gods, within this little frame,
Are warring night and day.

Heaven could not hold them all, and yet
They all are held in me
And must be mine till I forget
My present entity.

O for the time, when in my breast
Their struggles will be o'er;
O for the day when I shall rest,
And never suffer more!

"I saw a Spirit, standing, Man,
Where thou dost stand — an hour ago;
And round his feet, three rivers ran
Of equal depth, and equal flow —

"A Golden stream, and one like blood;
And one like sapphire, seemed to be,
But where they joined their triple flood
It tumbled in an inky sea.

"The Spirit bent his dazzling gaze
Down on that Ocean's gloomy night,
Then — kindling all with sudden blaze,
The glad deep sparkled wide and bright —
White as the sun; far, far more fair
Than the divided sources were!"

— And even for that Spirit, Seer,
I've watched and sought my lifetime long;
Sought Him in Heaven, Hell, Earth and Air,
An endless search — and always wrong!

Had I but seen his glorious eye
Once light the clouds that 'wilder me,
I ne'er had raised this coward cry
To cease to think and cease to be —

I ne'er had called oblivion blest,
Nor stretching eager hands to Death
Implored to change for lifeless rest
This sentient soul, this living breath.

Oh, let me die, that power and will
Their cruel strife may close,
And vanquished Good, and conquering Ill
Be lost in one repose.

"Enough of Thought, Philosopher" includes a mystical vision similar to that in the preceding poem. A "Philosopher" has had such an experience and he describes it with precision and certainty, including the exact spot and time it occurred. The only possible doubt of the reality of the vision is cast by the other speaker, a "Man," who notes in the first stanza that the Philosopher has been "dreaming." That one little doubt holds no sway over the rest of the poem, as both take the vision as true.

Looking at the structural progression of the poem to gain a clear understanding of the conversation, the Man starts the poem, addressing the Philosopher. The Man asks for a "refrain," the sum of the Philosopher's musings. The refrain, conveyed in the italicized stanzas, amounts to a desire for death. In it, the Philosopher admits to possessing wild desires and "a quenchless will." Those traits seem to plague him, given that he has just stated that he yearns for death. Brontë in another poem refers to curbing her "wild will." In "All day I've toiled, but not with pain," the speaker aspires to "turn away from passion's call / And curb my own wild will." The notion in these two poems that will and earthly desires mar one's life also appears in other belief systems and philosophies that view passion, desire, and will as impediments to living a spiritual or tranquil life. The Man rejoins that he is like-minded; he too yearns for death as an end to his struggles. The Philosopher then, apparently inspired by the Man's statement that *"three* Gods" are at war within him, relates his vision of *three* rivers and a celestial Spirit that he had just an hour earlier. Strangely, his vision of the spirit has not brightened his outlook or increased the value of life, although for the Man seeing such a vision would have made all the difference. What does the vision mean? We might prefer the other spirit from the previous poem who was perfectly clear in saying that life was a tomb and death glorious. All we have here are three streams that blend into a sea. Given that reaching the shore or crossing over an expanse of water frequently represents dying, there is some reason to see diverse currents of life all flowing into a great beyond that is fair and bright, i.e. a vague, yet apparently divine eternity. I have never satisfied myself as to why they are golden, blood, and sapphire. Given the importance of quenchless desires, each stream might represent a desire, as would each of the three "gods" warring in the Man's "little frame." The end of the vision offers the prospect of a fair, sparkling, and bright eternity; however the poem gives and then takes away. That promise of eternity comforts only if one can manage to believe it. The Man cannot because he has not had the experience himself. And even for the Philosopher, the comfort it offers can only be redeemed after death, as during life one will remain painfully subject to the will and unquenchable desires.

> **Well hast thou spoken — and yet not taught**
> A feeling strange or new;
> Thou hast but roused a latent thought,
> A cloud-closed beam of sunshine brought
> To gleam in open view.

Deep down — concealed within my soul,
That light lies hid from men,
Yet glows unquenched — though shadows roll,
Its gentle ray can not control —
About the sullen den.

Was I not vexed, in these gloomy ways
To walk unlit so long?
Around me, wretches uttering praise,
Or howling o'er their hopeless days,
And each with Frenzy's tongue —

A Brotherhood of misery,
With smiles as sad as sighs;
Their madness daily maddening me,
And turning into agony
The Bliss before my eyes.

So stood I, in Heaven's glorious sun
And in the glare of Hell
My spirit drank a mingled tone
Of seraph's song and demon's moan —
What my soul bore my soul alone
Within its self may tell.

Like a soft air above a sea
Tossed by the tempest's stir —
A thaw-wind melting quietly
The snowdrift on some wintery lea;
No — what sweet thing can match with thee,
My thoughtful Comforter?

And yet a little longer speak,
Calm this resentful mood,
And while the savage heart grows meek,
For other tokens do not seek,

But let the tear upon my cheek
Evince my gratitude.

"Well hast thou spoken — and yet not taught" introduces the
idea of a comforter, and the poem is entitled, "My Comforter." The
speaker addresses someone or something at the outset, and we learn
its identity in the sixth stanza as "My thoughtful Comforter."
There is a before and after to the speaker's spiritual life: at one time
she knew vexation, misery, and the torment of not being able to
reconcile heaven's glories and the glare of hell. Then, her comforter
ignites a peaceful and consoling thought that she has harbored
within herself all along and brings it to the surface. The fact that
the saving thought has been within her all along furthers the
notion that we have been tracing of an inner, self-sufficient system
of spirituality. Here, the "wretches uttering praise" and the utterly
worthless creeds in the poem "No coward Soul is mine" signify that
expressions of faith in the outside world only provoke disdain.

How beautiful the Earth is still
To thee — how full of Happiness;
How little fraught with real ill
Or shadowy phantoms of distress;

How Spring can bring thee glory yet
And Summer win thee to forget
December's sullen time!
Why dost thou hold the treasure fast
Of youth's delight, when youth is past
And thou art near thy prime?

When those who were thy own compeers,
Equal in fortunes and in years,
Have seen their morning melt in tears,
To dull unlovely day;
Blest, had they died unproved and young
Before their hearts were wildly wrung,

Poor slaves, subdued by passions strong,
A weak and helpless prey!

"Because, I hoped while they enjoyed,
And by fulfilment, hope destroyed —
As children hope, with trustful breast,
I waited Bliss and cherished Rest.

"A thoughtful Spirit taught me soon
That we must long till life be done;
That every phase of earthly joy
Will always fade and always cloy —

"This I foresaw, and would not chase
The fleeting treacheries,
But with firm foot and tranquil face
Held backward from the tempting race,
Gazed o'er the sands the waves efface
To the enduring seas —

"There cast my anchor of Desire
Deep in unknown Eternity;
Nor ever let my Spirit tire
With looking for *What is to be.*

"It is Hope's spell that glorifies
Like youth to my maturer eyes
All Nature's million mysteries —
The fearful and the fair —

"Hope soothes me in the griefs I know,
She lulls my pain for others' woe
And makes me strong to undergo
What I am born to bear.

"Glad comforter, will I not brave
Unawed the darkness of the grave?
Nay, smile to hear Death's billows rave,
My Guide, sustained by thee?
The more unjust seems present fate
The more my Spirit springs elate
Strong in thy strength, to anticipate
Rewarding Destiny!

"How beautiful the earth is still" presents two unidentified speakers, the first posing a question and the second answering. Both speakers agree that life, past youth, holds no redeeming features. That statement on the insufficiency of life recalls the poems on mutability that depict the changes after childhood as unhappy ones and reiterates the perception in so many poems that distress, sorrow, and passion plague mortal existence. The previous two poems in particular emphasized the harmful effects of passions and the will, and the captivity poem "Listen! when your hair like mine" treated the same idea, that indulging passion leads to misery. In this poem, although the two speakers agree on the lamentable state of life, they differ in their reactions. The first evinces amazement at the second persona's tranquility. All of the quoted stanzas contain the second speaker's explanation of how she has achieved her peaceful state of mind. First, she has realized and accepted the true nature of life: pursuing pleasure, succumbing to passion, and joining in treacheries lead to unhappiness. A "thoughtful Spirit" has taught her that lesson, although she has also come across it on her own. The essence of the Spirit's lesson that "every phase of earthly joy / will always fade and always cloy" echoes so nicely the same thought expressed by John Keats in "Ode on a Grecian Urn." He compares the unrealizable and static scene on the urn to earthly passion, finding passion inferior and insidiously flawed because it ". . . leaves a heart high-sorrowful and cloy'd, / A burning forehead, and a parching tongue."

The nature of the "thoughtful Spirit" appears like a personified emotion (like Hope in "Hope was but a timid friend") rather than a visitant; however, that Spirit does seem more like a distinct entity, separate from the speaker, when compared to the other spirit, "my Spirit," referred to in the lines "Nor ever let my Spirit tire / With looking for *What is to be*." Whereas the thoughtful Spirit has taught a lesson about life (one that she already has discovered), Hope does much more. As discussed in the chapter "Hope and Despair," in Brontë's poetic world hope can pertain to an improvement in earthly life or the prospect of something after life — here hope applies to the latter. With hope for what is to be, the speaker can see nature as glorious, bear grief and pain, and face death unperturbed. She also denominates Hope "Glad comforter" and her "Guide" imparting even more of a sense of what having hope is like — a feeling of security and trustworthy companionship.

The reference to a spirit and a rewarding destiny make this poem a clear statement on spiritual matters, and, in message and tone, the poem unreservedly rejoices in the steadfast understanding of the truth about life and death; however, there are vague elements. The declaration that something awaits beyond the grave is unequivocal, but the nature of that afterlife remains undescribed except that it promises to be rewarding. Most mystifying is the source of the sustaining hope because personifying Hope skirts an explanation of its real nature and origins. Hope has not actually appeared as a full bodied form; the speaker has not heard voices and celestial music. Judging from the tenor of Brontë's poetry as a whole, I would posit that in this poem Hope has come from within herself, in particular from her proclivity to imagine and even envision other worlds beyond reality and an existence unchained from mortal life.

This poem recounts a very personal approach to dealing with life and facing death that has philosophical tones in its view of life and the harmfulness of passion as well as religious chords in its exultation in a destiny beyond the grave. In its reiteration of ideas from previous poems, singularity, tone, and directness, this poem sounds like the poetic encapsulation of Brontë's own convictions, lending some biographical insights on Brontë's religious views. The poem does not implicate Christianity; most notably she never mentions the word "God," depicts a traditional heaven, or relies on any source except her own mind. From this poem and all the foregoing on imagination and spirituality, which I take as self-expressive, I would conclude that Brontë did not embrace traditional religion and it would appear that she attended church services throughout her life that did not console, instruct, or express her own beliefs. No wonder there is such a force to her poetic declarations — they address a lifetime of dissatisfaction with practices that she was outwardly compelled to follow. In her poems, time and again, she throws down the gantlet of self-reliance and self-sufficiency, stating that she has developed her own understanding, has her own comforter, and is answering her own prayers. Nonetheless, when considering how a reader might appropriate a poem as his or her own spiritual source, as advocated in the Introduction to this book, I would think that any Christian would embrace this poem as an apt and eloquent expression of faith. Thanks to the malleability of words and the techniques of personification and metaphor, poetic lines can answer different callings.

This is a wonderful poem on which to end not only because it is a manifesto of Brontë's beliefs on topics of the deepest human importance, but also because it brings to a crescendo the various strains in so many of her poems: an appreciation of nature; the dire state of Man's existence; hope for something more than grim reality; the need to reconcile life and death; the beauty of the world within, and the power of the mind. We can rightly conclude that she had recourse to the anthem precepts of this poem in facing the vicissitudes of life and the unknown of death.

Conclusion

I have on several occasions in this book noted that Emily Brontë was influenced by Byron's poetry. In exploring that influence, I happily got to know Byron more than hitherto, and I am now reminded of the closing lines of "Childe Harold" as the best of all possible words to conclude a written work:

> My task is done — my song hath ceased — my theme
> Has died into an echo; it is fit
> The spell should break of this protracted dream,
> The torch shall be extinguished which hath lit
> My midnight lamp — and what is writ is writ
> Would it were worthier!

In my case, the task rested upon a few assumptions that started the project. It seemed to me that Emily Brontë had not received her due as a poet. She certainly had not been recognized during her lifetime, or for many years after; however, I did not initially even know of the historical neglect. I simply thought that if I, who had read Romantic and Victorian poets, was not even aware that Emily Brontë wrote poetry, the same could be said for many others. The second assumption was that segments of the population would enjoy her poetry. I surmised, however, that there might be impediments to that enjoyment: the reluctance many people have to reading poetry generally and whatever there is of arcane or peculiar about Brontë's poetry in particular. I remember when I first encountered a few of her poems, I felt nonplussed by many lines. From that point of curiosity, I studied the poems, *Wuthering*

Heights, biography of all the Brontës, and ancillary poets to arrive at my great appreciation of her work. My goal was to kindle in others some degree of similar fervor.

My process necessarily excluded other important elements, and I will mention avenues of investigation not pursued, in case one might find them of interest. First, I did not discuss Brontë's meter and rhyme schemes, but I value the musicality of her lines and how rhythm and rhyme serve to convey ideas and emotion. Meter and rhyme make so many phrases cling to one's mind, and those tools are a necessary cause for the poetic effect in Brontë's poems (and, I would say, in poetry generally). Somewhere along the dubious path of innovation, meter and rhyme disappeared. Has there been an improvement in making poetry like prose? Certainly more people can now have a go at writing it. For me, a poem should have an important idea and the meter and rhyme to make the expression of that idea memorable. Rhyme might not be critical — "Paradise Lost" and Shakespeare's plays attest to that, although they do have meter; however, an exception for epic poems and plays is not a justifiable precedent for calling "poetry" miscellaneous effusions of short prose, however elliptical or cryptic they might be.

The second subject beyond the scope of this book was literary criticism. When I gave an interpretation of a poem, it was solely my own, as I was not synthesizing other scholars who propose various interpretations, as they are wont to do. Also, one can read scholarly research that builds a case for influences on Brontë, such as German literature, fairy tales, and Wordsworth or for Brontë's influence on or similarity to other poets, such as Emily Dickinson. Although I have alluded to certain influences, the focus has been on Brontë's words in context and not on what others have said about them either as the heir to or progenitor of other poetry. Likewise, scholars frequently investigate the time and place of a poem's creation either to make sense of it as a Gondal plot incident or to associate it with a phase in Brontë's life, such as when she was at Roe Head, Law Hill, or Brussels (her three boarding school experiences, either as a student or a teacher, excluding

Cowan Bridge which she attended as a little child). I have strongly suggested the poems stand alone without an understanding of the Gondal background, and the approach of studying the poems as reflections of stages in Brontë's life must confront the great dearth of information about Brontë — an insurmountable impediment in my view.

I have discussed *Wuthering Heights* frequently because it figures greatly as part of Brontë's poetic world: themes, images, and diction in the poems and novel blend together. Also, there is poetry in *Wuthering Heights*. In my view, the novel contains lines and sections that read more like poetry than most modern poetry; however, it is also graced with a fast and intriguing narrative, so it is easy for a reader to fly over the poetry, like Isabella flying over the moors toward Thrushcross Grange when she finally makes her escape. Taking note of the poetic language might enhance a future reading of the novel. A parting thought on *Wuthering Heights*: it remains a great mystery to me why there has not been a cinematic version of that book that is true to it. One that starts at the beginning, follows the narrative to the end, and gives us each character as written: Lockwood, Nelly Dean, Joseph, Francis Earnshaw, Linton Heathcliff, even Dr. Kenneth — those characters who are omitted in the movie and made-for-television versions that fixate on a love story and then fail to present even that in keeping with the book.

I would like, and have no doubt, that some readers have found new friends among her poems, having come upon the surprising expression of a familiar feeling, the resonance of a lyrical phrase, the innovative articulation of an idea, or the discovery of a thought similar to one of another beloved poet. Equally, I count on having imparted something of Brontë's identity. I hope that the biographical information has made an impression not only because it adds to understanding the poems, but also because Emily Brontë presents so many points of interest: she was equally a poet and a novelist, faced a restrictive era with an independent spirit, possessed genius, and figured as a member of a most unusual family.

Such was the task. As to its worthiness, if a few, even one, take half as much pleasure from reading this as I did in writing it, it is worthy enough.

Story Poems

Today when we consider poetry, reading it or writing it, we most likely mean a lyric poem: a personal expression of a state of mind, feeling, or perception that is of fairly short length. Most of Emily Brontë's poems are of the lyric genre. The first part of the definition, personal expression, implicates narration, since the idea of a personal expression connotes a first person narrator. The genre does, however, encompass more than a simple first person narration in the poet's own voice. Brontë's poetry provides strong evidence of the diversity possible, as she wrote lyric poems that do not necessarily convey her own feelings, at least on their face. As we have seen in this book, there are poems in the first person, but that feature a speaker (not ostensibly the poet herself) delivering a dramatic monologue or addressing others, directly or rhetorically; other poems are in the third person, like an observer; some even in the second person. Many poems are told through a conversation between two speakers or by one speaker taking up two sides of a question. All those poems depict some persona's view, thought process, or mindset on a topic, in accordance with the genre of lyric poetry. As for the second criterion of the genre, her poems are not long for the most part, considering the length of epic poetry and many poetic works from the Romantic era.

Brontë's poems, as mostly lyric works centered on an idea, have lent themselves to the topical system of this book. However, other poems by Brontë are not so much lyric poems as story poems and, although they do present themes (just as any work of fiction would), they do not fit within the topical framework as neatly. Nonetheless, they should not be missed, as they fill in the landscape of Brontë's poetic world. By a story poem, I mean one in which interest in the narrative and characters constitutes, like in a novel or short story, an integral and essential part of a poem of several pages. In such works we encounter characters that have depth and that develop, and plots that progress in time and that interest the reader in the outcome of the tale.

Brontë departed from the lyric poem to write story poems very naturally for two reasons. First, it does not appear that she gave much thought to poetic genre, unlike other poets. As a contrasting example, John Keats (although he insisted that he wrote for himself and hated a "mawkish popularity") had to write for the public and considered what genre to pursue as striking the right chord with an audience — long or short, lyric or narrative, a sonnet or song. Brontë was writing for herself, and the length and form of a poem just seem malleable and variable according to inspiration. Second, it stands to reason that she would set a scene and tell a story because she was also a novelist and inveterate creator of fictional characters and stories as part of the Gondal world. In telling a story, just as in prose, some greater length is needed; therefore these poems are longer than typical lyric expressions. Taking a look at other poets of the era, the length of a poem poses a more interesting literary question than it might first appear. Keats queried whether his audience might want to spend time wandering around in a long poem, then felt that a short poem might be more to most people's taste. When Keats tried to revive the epic, with his epic, theme-driven poem, *Hyperion*, he abandoned it. Various reasons came into play, but maybe quitting it was a sign of the times — the long poem was losing vogue. However, when it came to telling a story, just as in prose, a certain length was required, and Keats had success with long poems when he told the story of Lamia and Lucius in "Lamia" and of Isabella and Lorenzo in "Isabella." Coleridge also needed many pages to tell his tales. Byron told the adventures of Don Juan at great length (although that work is as much concerned with satirical commentary on the age and Byron's acquaintances as with the exploits of the famous lover). Whether Brontë needed or even thought of any of those near contemporaries as precedent for a poem with plot, character development, and expanded length, she wrote three poems that I consider story poems, which appear below. I have noted that there is poetry in *Wuthering Heights*, and now we see stories in her poems.

Consideration of genre aside, our focus can turn to the nature of her stories. One of her longest poems tells a vivid and compelling tale in a battle setting. Many of her poems, whatever the genre designation, unfurl a battle backdrop. Why did Brontë gravitate toward a battle setting? If she had been an artist would she have deviated from pastorals and portraits and painted scenes of gory slaughter? She was artistic and did draw very well (all three of the sisters drew and Branwell had for a time made a small living as a portrait artist). Her graphic art shows drawings of trees and animals, sketches of her sisters, and one curious depiction of the Christian ascetic, Simeon Stylites. Looking at biography for an answer, famous battles were topics of conversation around the parsonage, as the household revered Lord Wellington and followed closely current events. Also, all of the Brontë children played with toy soldiers that Mr. Brontë had bought for Branwell, and they created stories around them. That experience led to the creation of Gondal, which she and Anne pursued throughout their lives, and Gondal itself includes many battles. Leaving biography and taking a writer's standpoint, a battle gave her a large canvass to depict action and emotion, in particular, human nature at its cruelest and then, concomitantly, its most remorseful, with large doses of anguish and suffering, and the possibility of bravery or virtue. Such is the panoply of emotion offered in the poem "Why ask to know the date, the clime."

Warring factions also provide the background to the poem "Silent is the House — all are laid asleep," entitled, "Julian M. and A.G. Rochelle." However, most of the narrative happens away from battle in that place so frequently visited in her poems, a dungeon. The characters, through their words and actions, express two themes that will also seem familiar after having read the poems presented in this book: death is the welcome end to suffering and childhood is the basis for enduring affection. Also, the spiritual experience described by the prisoner, beginning with the line, "He comes with western wind, with evening's wandering airs," will seem very familiar: night time and the wind bring spiritual visions that comfort and promise a blissful eternity.

This poem also presents elements that call to mind *Wuthering Heights*. The motifs of captivity and freedom and the appeal of death, mentioned above with regard to this poem's kinship with other poems, also create a link to *Wuthering Heights*, as does the idea that associations formed in childhood are the most binding. Another connection to *Wuthering Heights* appears in the story-line of the poem: two young people develop an affection originating in childhood that ends in death, suggestive of Heathcliff and Catherine. Third and most interesting, the narrative structure of this poem makes it a fledging precursor to that novel. Both the poem and the novel are structured as a flashback, starting with the introduction of events and people that leave the reader curious. From the first stanzas of the poem, one does not know why and for whom the narrator is watching and lighting a beacon. Likewise, in *Wuthering Heights*, the reader encounters in the early chapters characters and situations that are strange and curious, just as they appear to the newcomer to the area, Mr. Lockwood. Both narratives also contain a second level of flashback to relate incidents from the earlier period of childhood. In the poem, the protagonist and the captive harken back to their childhood together when they become aware of the shared past. In *Wuthering Heights*, the flashback is accomplished first through Catherine's writing in the book that Lockwood comes across in the paneled bed then later through Nelly Dean's account to Lockwood. The chronology in both works is specific: in the poem, thirteen weeks marks a measure of time and the seasons indicate the passage of time; in the novel, dates and seasons mark the passage of time very precisely to situate the events of the story over many years. As for the number of weeks mentioned in the poem, I have to wonder why thirteen weeks. I have discussed in earlier parts of this book my theory that Brontë used the numbers two and twelve symbolically in *Wuthering Heights* to represent death, and I have my suspicions about this number thirteen. Of course, it is the standard unlucky number, but maybe it enjoys an even greater and recondite significance in Brontë's world.

The third story poem, "And now the house-dog stretched once more," presents a rather superficial, yet interesting, tie to *Wuthering Heights* with the appearance of a dog. In the novel, dogs galore grace the pages: several inhabit the corners and dark recesses of the "house" at Wuthering Heights and emerge to greet and then attack Lockwood. A dog threatens and then befriends Isabella when she takes up residence at Wuthering Heights. Isabella has a dog that Heathcliff hangs as they are about to elope. Edgar Linton and Isabella Linton, as children, are playing with a puppy in the comfort of their drawing room when Heathcliff and Catherine spy upon them. A dog bites Catherine Earnshaw's foot, causing her to stay at Thrushcross Grange, which, by the way, triggers a significant plot development.

Given Brontë's proclivity to include dogs in her novel and her own dog ownership, I am almost surprised that this is the only poem that features a dog (with one minor exception: in the poem "From our evening fireside now" hunting dogs pine at the absence of the deceased). Brontë's dog, Keeper, was her close companion, and the story is told how Keeper accompanied the family to church on the day of Brontë's funeral, lay quietly through the service, and lived for many years bereft. In the poem, although the presence of the dog helps set the scene, the poem moves on to depict a mysterious visitor, and in that, suggests a character sketch for a bigger work, again, *Wuthering Heights*. A traveler out of nowhere, with a sinister air, appears at a farm, reminding one of Heathcliff when he returns as a grown man, from where and having done what nobody knows, but inexplicably changed. An alternative view of this poem and my parting thought, in a familiar strain: might the chilling guest in the poem be the same unwelcome visitor as in the poem "I'll come when thou art saddest"?

Why ask to know the date the clime?
More than mere words they cannot be:
Men knelt to God and worshipped crime,
And crushed the helpless even as we.

But they had learnt, from length of strife
Of civil war and anarchy,
To laugh at death and look on life
With somewhat lighter sympathy.

It was the autumn of the year,
The time to labouring peasants dear;
Week after week, from noon to noon,
September shone as bright as June —
Still, never hand a sickle held;
The crops were garnered in the field —
Trod out and ground by horse's feet
While every ear was milky sweet;
And kneaded on the threshing floor
With mire of tears and human gore.
Some said they thought that heaven's pure rain
Would hardly bless those fields again:
Not so — the all-benignant skies
Rebuked that fear of famished eyes
July passed on with showers and dew,
And August glowed in showerless blue;
No harvest time could be more fair
Had harvest fruits but ripened there.

And I confess that hate of rest,
And thirst for things abandoned now,
Had weaned me from my country's breast
And brought me to that land of woe.

Enthusiast — in a name delighting,
My alien sword I drew to free

One race, beneath two standards, fighting
For Loyalty and Liberty —

When kindred strive — God help the weak!
A brother's ruth 'tis vain to seek:
At first, it hurt my chivalry
To join them in their cruelty;
But I grew hard — I learnt to wear
An iron front to terror's prayer;
I learnt to turn my ears away
From torture's groans as well as they.
By force I learnt — what power had I
To say the conquered should not die?
What heart, one trembling foe to save
When hundreds daily filled the grave?
Yet there *were* faces that could move
A moment's flash of human love;
And there were fates that made me feel
I was not, to the centre steel —

I've often witnessed wise men fear
To meet distress which they foresaw;
And seeming cowards nobly bear
A doom that thrilled the brave with awe.

Strange proofs I've seen, how hearts could hide
Their secret with a lifelong pride,
And then reveal it as they died —
Strange courage, and strange weakness too,
In that last hour when most are true,
And timid natures strangely nerved
To deeds from which the desperate swerved.
These I may tell; but, leave them now:
Go with me where my thoughts would go;
Now all to-day and all last night
I've had one scene before my sight —

Wood-shadowed dales, a harvest moon
Unclouded in its glorious noon;
A solemn landscape wide and still;
A red fire on a distant hill —
A line of fires, and deep below
Another duskier, drearier glow —
Charred beams, and lime, and blackened stones
Self-piled in cairns o'er burning bones,
And lurid flames that licked the wood,
Then quenched their glare in pools of blood.

But yester-eve — No! never care;
Let street and suburb smoulder there —
Smoke-hidden, in the winding glen
They lay too far to vex my ken.

Four score shot down — all veterans strong;
One prisoner spared — their leader — young,
And he within his house was laid
Wounded, and weak and nearly dead.
We gave him life against his will,
For he entreated us to kill —
And statue-like we saw his tears —
And harshly fell our captain's sneers!

"Now, heaven forbid!" with scorn he said,
"That noble gore our hands should shed
Like common blood — retain thy breath,
Or scheme, if thou canst purchase death.
When men are poor we sometimes hear
And pitying grant that dastard prayer;
When men are rich we make them buy
The pleasant privilege to die.
O, we have castles reared for kings,
Embattled towers and buttressed wings
Thrice three feet thick, and guarded well

With chain and bolt and sentinel!
We build our despots' dwellings sure
Knowing they love to live secure —
And our respect for royalty
Extends to thy estate and thee!"

The supplicant groaned; his moistened eye
Swam wild and dim with agony.
The gentle blood could ill sustain
Degrading taunts, unhonoured pain.

Bold had he shown himself to lead;
Eager to smite and proud to bleed;
A man amid the battle's storm:
An infant in the after calm.

Beyond the town his mansion stood
Girt round with pasture-land and wood;
And there our wounded soldiers lying
Enjoyed the ease of wealth in dying.

For him, no mortal more then he
Had softened life with luxury;
And truly did our priest declare
"Of good things he had had his share."

We lodged him in an empty place,
The full moon beaming on his face
Through shivered glass, and ruins, made
Where shell and ball the fiercest played.

I watched his ghastly couch beside
Regardless if he lived or died —
Nay, muttering curses on the breast
Whose ceaseless moans denied me rest.
'Twas hard, I know, 'twas harsh to say

"Hell snatch thy worthless soul away!"
But then 'twas hard my lids to keep
Through this long night estranged from sleep.
Captive and keeper, both outworn
Each in his misery yearned for morn,
Even though returning morn should bring
Intenser toil and suffering.

Slow, slow it came! Our dreary room
Grew drearier with departing gloom;
Yet as the west wind warmly blew
I felt my pulses bound anew,
And turned to him — Nor breeze, nor ray
Revived that mould of shattered clay.
Scarce conscious of his pain he lay —
Scarce conscious that my hands removed
The glittering toys his lightness loved —
The jewelled rings and locket fair
Where rival curls of silken hair
Sable and brown revealed to me
A tale of doubtful constancy.

"Forsake the world without regret,"
I murmured in contemptuous tone;
"The world poor wretch will soon forget
Thy noble name when thou art gone!
Happy, if years of slothful shame
Could perish like a noble name —
If God did no account require
And being with breathing might expire!"
And words of such contempt I said,
Harsh insults o'er a dying bed,
Which as they darken memory now
Disturb my pulse and flush my brow.
I know that Justice holds in store
Reprisals for these days of gore;

Not for the blood, but for the sin
Of stifling mercy's voice within.

The blood spilt gives no pang at all;
It is my conscience haunting me,
Telling how oft my lips shed gall
On many a thing too weak to be,
Even in thought, my enemy;
And whispering ever, when I pray,
"God will repay — God will repay!"

He does repay and soon and well
The deeds that turn his earth to hell,
The wrongs that aim a venomed dart
Through nature at the Eternal Heart.
Surely my cruel tongue was cursed
I know my prisoner heard me speak
A transient gleam of feeling burst
And wandered o'er his haggard cheek
And from his quivering lids there stole
A look to melt a demon's soul
A silent prayer more powerful far
Then any breathed petitions are
Pleading in mortal agony
To mercy's Source but not to me.
Now I recall that glance and groan
And wring my hands in vain distress;
Then I was adamantine stone
Nor felt one touch of tenderness.

My plunder ta'en I left him there
Without one breath of morning air
To struggle with his last despair,
Regardless of the 'wildered cry
Which wailed for death, yea wailed to die.
I left him there unwatched, alone,

And eager sought the court below
Where o'er a trough of chiselled stone
An ice cold well did gurgling flow.
The water in its basin shed
A stranger tinge of fiery red.
I drank and scarcely marked the hue;
My food was dyed with crimson too.
As I went out, a ragged child
With wasted cheek and ringlets wild,
A shape of fear and misery,
Raised up her helpless hands to me
And begged her father's face to see.
I spurned the piteous wretch away
"Thy fathers face is lifeless clay
As thine mayst be ere fall of day
Unless the truth be quickly told —
Where have they hid thy father's gold."
Yet in the intervals of pain
He heard my taunts and moaned again
And mocking moans did I reply
And asked him why he would not die
In noble agony — uncomplaining.
Was it not foul disgrace and shame
To thus disgrace his ancient name?

Just then a comrade hurried in
"Alas," he cried, "sin genders sin
For every soldier slain they've sworn
To hang up five to-morrow morn.
They've ta'en of stranglers sixty three,
Full thirty from one company,
And all my father's family
And comrade thou hadst only one —
They've ta'en thy all, thy little son."
Down at my captive's feet I fell

I had no option in despair
"As thou wouldst save thy soul from hell
My heart's own darling bid them spare
Or human hate and hate divine
Blight every orphan flower of thine."
He raised his head — from death beguiled,
He wakened up — he almost smiled
"I lost last night my only child
Twice in my arms twice on my knee
You stabbed my child and laughed at me
And so," with chocking voice he said
"I trust in God I hope she's dead
Yet not to thee, not even to thee
Would I return such misery.
Such is that fearful grief I know
I will not cause thee equal woe
Write that they harm no infant there
Write that it is my latest prayer."
I wrote — he signed — and thus did save
My treasure from the gory grave
And O my soul longed wildly then
To give his saviour life again.
But heedless of my gratitude
The silent corpse before me lay
And still methinks in gloomy mood
I see it fresh as yesterday
The sad face raised imploringly
To mercy's God and not to me.
I could not rescue him; his child
I found alive, and tended well
But she was full of anguish wild
And hated me like we hate hell
And weary with her savage woe
One moonless night I let her go.

Silent is the House — all are laid asleep;
One, alone, looks out o'er the snow wreaths deep;
Watching every cloud, dreading every breeze
That whirls the 'wildering drifts and bends the groaning trees.

Cheerful is the hearth, soft the matted floor;
Not one shivering gust creeps through pane or door;
The little lamp burns straight, its rays shoot strong and far;
I trim it well to be the Wanderer's guiding-star.

Frown, my haughty sire; chide, my angry dame;
Set your slaves to spy, threaten me with shame:
But neither sire nor dame, nor prying serf shall know
What angel nightly tracks that waste of winter snow.

In the dungeon crypts idly did I stray,
Reckless of the lives wasting there away;
"Draw the ponderous bars; open, Warder stern!"
He dare not say me nay — the hinges harshly turn.

"Our guests are darkly lodged," I whispered, gazing through
The vault whose grated eye showed heaven more grey than blue.
(This was when glad spring laughed in awaking pride.)
"Aye, darkly lodged enough!" returned my sullen guide.

Then, God forgive my youth, forgive my careless tongue!
I scoffed, as the chill chains on the damp flagstones rung;
"Confined in triple walls, art thou so much to fear,
That we must bind thee down and clench thy fetters here?"

The captive raised her face; it was as soft and mild
As sculptured marble saint or slumbering, unweaned child;
It was so soft and mild, it was so sweet and fair,
Pain could not trace a line nor grief a shadow there!

The captive raised her hand and pressed it to her brow:
"I have been struck," she said, "and I am suffering now;
Yet these are little worth, your bolts and irons strong;
And were they forged in steel they could not hold me long."

Hoarse laughed the jailor grim: "Shall I be won to hear;
Dost think, fond dreaming wretch, that *I* shall grant
    thy prayer?
Or, better still, wilt melt my master's heart with groans?
Ah, sooner might the sun thaw down these granite stones!

"My master's voice is low, his aspect bland and kind,
But hard as hardest flint the soul that lurks behind;
And I am rough and rude, yet not more rough to see
Than is the hidden ghost which has its home in me!

About her lips there played a smile of almost scorn:
"My friend," she gently said, "you have not heard me mourn;
When you my parents' lives — *my* lost life, can restore,
Then may I weep and sue — but *never*, Friend, before!"

Her head sank on her hands; its fair curls swept the ground;
The dungeon seemed to swim in strange confusion round —
"Is she so near to death?" I murmured, half aloud,
And, kneeling, parted back the floating golden cloud.

Alas, how former days upon my hear were borne;
How memory mirrored then the prisoner's joyous morn;
Too blithe, too loving child, too warmly, wildly gay!
Was that the wintry close of thy celestial May?

She knew me and she sighed, "Lord Julian, can it be,
Of all my playmates, you alone remember me?
Nay, start not at my words, unless you deem it shame
To own, from conquered foe, a once-familiar name.

"I cannot wonder now at ought the world will do,
And insult and contempt I lightly brook from you,
Since those, who vowed away their souls to win my love,
Around this living grave like utter strangers move!

"Nor has one voice been raised to plead that I might die,
Not buried under earth but in the open sky;
By ball or speedy knife or headsman's skillful blow —
A quick and welcome pang instead of lingering woe!

"Yet, tell them, Julian, all, I am not doomed to wear
Year after year in gloom and desolate despair;
A messenger of Hope comes every night to me,
And offers, for short life, eternal liberty.

He comes with western winds, with evening's wandering
    airs,
With that clear dusk of heaven that brings the thickest stars;
Winds take a pensive tone, and stars a tender fire,
And visions rise and change which kill me with desire —

"Desire for nothing known in my maturer years
When joy grew mad with awe at counting future tears;
When, if my spirit's sky was full of flashes warm,
I knew not whence they came, from sun or thunderstorm;

"But first a hush of peace, a soundless calm descends;
The struggle of distress and fierce impatience ends;
Mute music soothes my breast — unuttered harmony
That I could never dream till earth was lost to me.

"Then dawns the Invisible, the Unseen its truth reveals;
My outward sense is gone, my inward essence feels —
Its wings are almost free, its home, its harbour found;
Measuring the gulf it stoops and dares the final bound!

"Oh, dreadful is the check — intense the agony
When the ear begins to hear and the eye begins to see;
When the pulse begins to throb, the brain to think again,
The soul to feel the flesh and the flesh to feel the chain!

"Yet I would lose no sting, would wish no torture less;
The more that anguish racks the earlier it will bless;
And robed in fires of Hell, or bright with heavenly shine,
If it but herald Death, the vision is divine."

She ceased to speak, and I, unanswering, watched her there,
Not daring now to touch one lock of silken hair —
As I had knelt in scorn, on the dank floor I knelt still,
My fingers in the links of that iron hard and chill.

I heard, and yet heard not, the surly keeper growl;
I saw, yet did not see, the flagstone damp and foul.
The keeper, to and fro, paced by the bolted door
And shivered as he walked and, as he shivered, swore.

While my cheek glowed in flame, I marked that he did rave
Of air that froze his blood, and moisture like the grave —
"We have been two hours good!" he muttered peevishly;
Then, loosing off his belt the rusty dungeon key,

He said, "You may be pleased, Lord Julian, still to stay,
But duty will not let me linger here all day;
If I might go, I'd leave this badge of mine with you,
Not doubting that you'd prove a jailor stern and true."

I took the proffered charge, the captive's drooping lid
Beneath its shady lash a sudden lightening hid:
Earth's hope was not so dead, heaven's home was not
      so dear;
I read it in that flash of longing quelled by fear.

Then like a tender child whose hand did just enfold,
Safe in its eager grasp, a bird it wept to hold,
When pierced with one wild glance from the troubled hazel
    eye,
It gushes into tears and lets its treasure fly,

Thus ruth and selfish love together striving tore
The heart all newly taught to pity and adore;
If I should break the chain, I felt my bird would go;
Yet I must break the chain or seal the prisoner's woe.

Short strife, what rest could soothe — what peace could
    visit me
While she lay pining for Death to set her free?
"Rochelle, the dungeons teem with foes to gorge our hate —
Thou art too young to die by such a bitter fate!"

With hurried blow on blow, I struck the fetters through,
Regardless how that deed my after hours might rue.
Oh, I was over-blest by the warm unasked embrace —
By the smile of grateful joy that lit her angel face!

And I was over-blest — aye, more than I could dream
When, faint, she turned aside from noon's unwonted beam;
When though the cage was side — the heaven around it
    lay —
Its pinion would not waft my wounded dove away.

Through thirteen anxious week of terror-blent delight
I guarded her by day and guarded her by night,
While foes were prowling near and Death gazed greedily
And only Hope remained a faithful friend to me.

Then oft with taunting smile I heard my kindred tell
"How Julian loved his hearth and sheltering roof-tree
    well;

How trumpet's voice might call, the battle-standard
    wave,
But Julian had no heart to fill a patriot's grave."

And I, who am so quick to answer sneer with sneer;
So ready to condemn, to scorn, a coward's fear,
I held my peace like one whose conscience keeps him dumb,
And saw my kinsman go — and lingered still at home.

Another hand than mine my rightful banner held
And gathered my renown on Freedom's crimson field;
Yet I had no desire the glorious prize to gain —
It needed braver nerve to face the world's disdain.

And by the patient strength that could that world defy,
By suffering, with calm mind, contempt and calumny,
By never-doubting love, unswerving constancy,
Rochelle, I earned at last an equal love from thee!

And now the house-dog stretched once more
His limbs upon the glowing floor;
The children half resumed their play,
Though from the warm hearth scared away.
The goodwife left her spinning-wheel,
And spread with smiles the evening meal;
The shepherd placed a seat and pressed
To their poor fare his unknown guest.
And he unclasped his mantle now,
And raised the covering from his brow;
Said, "Voyagers by land and sea
Were seldom feasted daintily";
And checked his host by adding stern
He'd no refinement to unlearn.
A silence settled on the room;
The cheerful welcome sank to gloom;
But not those words, though cold and high,

So froze their hospitable joy.
No — there was something in his face,
Some nameless thing they could not trace,
And something in his voice's tone
Which tuned their blood as chill as stone.
The ringlets of his long black hair
Fell o'er a cheek most ghastly fair,
Youthful he seemed — but worn as they
Who spend too soon their youthful day.
When his glance drooped, 'twas hard to quell
Unbidden feelings' sudden swell;
And pity scarce her tears could hide,
So sweet that brow, with all its pride;
But when upraised his eye would dart
An icy shudder through the heart.
Compassion changed to horror then
And fear to meet that gaze again.
It was not hatred's tiger-glare,
Nor the wild anguish of despair;
It was not useless misery
Which mocks at friendship's sympathy.
No — lightning all unearthly shone
Deep in that dark eye's circling zone,
Such withering lightning as we deem
None but a spectre's look may beam;
And glad they were when he turned away
And wrapt him in his mantle grey,
Leant down his head upon his arm
And veiled from view their basilisk charm.

The Palace of Death

Below is my translation of an essay that Emily Brontë wrote while studying at the Pensionnat Heger in Brussels. Charlotte and Emily were in their twenties when they left Haworth with the intention of spending a year in Brussels learning French in order to teach French at the boarding school that Charlotte, Emily, and Anne wanted to establish at the parsonage. It was an exciting scheme for them, as it would provide a way to make a living while allowing them to remain together at home, and they devoted to the plan much preparation and effort. Ultimately, advertisements failed to yield even a single expression of interest in the school, and they were compelled to abandon the plan.

At the Pensionnat Heger, Charlotte and Emily took French lessons from the owner's husband, Constantin Heger, an experienced teacher of French. He taught French to Charlotte and Emily through the writing of creative essays, a method that he designed specifically for them. He thought that for these two older and foreign students he needed a different pedagogical approach, but little did he know just how perfect his method would prove for his two unusual students. It is not known exactly what the assignment was that led to this essay, "the Palace of Death" — whether Monsieur Heger designated the precise topic, gave some kind of precedent, or made a general suggestion. I have included this essay because it continues ideas that the poems have explored: the dire and lamentable state of the world and the awful power of death. It also shows personification, a poetic tool of frequent use by Brontë, in an elaborate and extended fashion. The thoughts expressed in this essay also presage the depiction of Hindley Earnshaw's downfall in *Wuthering Heights*. I hope that last observation has not spoiled the ending of the essay, and I must say no more that might do so.

THE PALACE OF DEATH

In the past, when men were few in number, Death lived frugally and with limited means. Her only minister was Old Age, who guarded the door of the palace and introduced from time to time a single victim to appease the hunger of her mistress: this abstinence was soon repaid; the prey of her majesty grew prodigiously, and Old Age began to find that she had too much to handle.

It was at this time that Death decided to change her manner of living, to appoint new agents, and take a prime minister. On the day appointed for the nomination, the silence of the somber palace was broken by the arrival of the candidates from all sides; the arch ways, the rooms, and the hallways resonated with the sound of the footsteps coming and going, as if the bones strewn on the paving stones were suddenly animated, and Death looked from above on her throne, and smiled hideously to see such a multitude running to serve her.

Among the first to come were Anger and Vengeance who went before her Majesty, arguing loudly about their respective rights; Envy and Betrayal took their places in the shadows; Hunger and Pestilence, assisted by their companions Laziness and Greed obtained comfortable spots among the crowd and threw disdainful glances on the other guests; however, they found themselves forced to make way when Ambition and Fanaticism appeared, the entourage of these two persons filling the council room, and they demanded imperiously a prompt audience.

"I do not doubt" said the first, "that your Majesty will be just in her decision so why waste the time in vain disputes when a quick glance is sufficient to determine the only one worthy of the office in question? What are all these pretenders who besiege your throne? What do they think they would do in your service? The most able among them could not govern your empire any more than a soldier who has no qualification except his bravery could command an army. They know how to strike down a victim here and another there, they can catch the feeble prey, men on whom your mark is visible from birth, and that is the extent of their usefulness; whereas for me, I will lead to your doors the elite of the race, those who are the farthest from your power; I will strike them in full flower and offer them to you in entire groups all at once. Then, I have so many methods; it is not only spears that win me victories; I have other helpers, secret, but powerful allies; Fanaticism herself is only one of the tools that I will employ."

In hearing these words, Fanaticism shook her savage head and rose up toward Death with a burning and maniacal eye and began:

"I know that this glorious one will easily borrow my weapons and march under my standards, but is that a reason that she would presume to compare herself with me? Not only will I be as powerful as she in overthrowing states and destroying kingdoms, I will enter into families; I will create opposition between son and father, daughter and mother; inspired by me, faithful friend will become mortal enemy, the wife will betray her husband, the servant his master; no feeling can resist me. I will travel the world under the light of the sky, and crowns will be like stones under my feet. As for the other candidates, they are not worthy of your consideration; Anger is irrational; Vengeance is partial; Hunger could be defeated by hard work; Pestilence is capricious. Your prime minister must be someone close to men and possess them; decide then between Ambition and me, we are the only ones you should consider."

Fanaticism fell silent, and her Majesty seemed in doubt as between these two rivals when the doors of the gallery opened and a person entered before whom everyone recoiled in surprise for she had an appearance which radiated joy and health. Her step was light as the wind, and Death herself seemed uneasy at her first approach; however, she soon felt reassured. "You know me" said the stranger, "I come later than the others, but I know that my cause is sure. Certain of my rivals are formidable, I admit, and it is possible that I could be surpassed in striking feats that attract the admiration of the vulgar, but I have a friend before whom everyone in this assembly would be forced to succumb; she is named Civilization. In a few years she will come to live on earth with you and each century her power will increase. In the end she will turn away Ambition from your service; she will throw on Anger the brakes of the law; she will uproot weapons from the hands of Fanaticism; she will hunt down Famine among the savages. I alone will increase and flourish under her regime. The power of all the others will expire with their supporters — mine will exist even when I am dead. If at one time I knew the father, my influence will extend to the son, and before men unite to banish me from their society, I will have changed their entire nature and rendered them a type entirely at the mercy of your Majesty, so effectively, that Old Age will have a sinecure and your palace will be filled up with victims."

"Speak no more" said Death descending from her throne and kissing Intemperance (for it is thus that the stranger was named). "It suffices that I know you; for the others I have valuable and important offices, they will all be my ministers, but to you alone is reserved the honor of my prince."

List of Poems by First Line

Bibliography

Brontë, Anne. *Agnes Grey*. London: Penguin Books, 1988.

Brontë, Charlotte. *Jane Eyre*. London: Penguin Books, 2006.

Brontë, Emily. *Wuthering Heights*. London: Penguin Books, 2003.

Brontë, Emily. *The Complete Poems of Emily Jane Brontë*. Edited by C.W. Hatfield. New York: Columbia University Press, 1947.

Byron, George Gordon Lord. *The Selected Poetry of Lord Byron*. Edited by Digireads.com. Publishing. www.digireads.com. 2009.

Chitham, Edward. *A Life of Emily Brontë*. Oxford: Clarendon Press, 1971.

Dinsdale, Ann. *The Brontës at Haworth*. London: Frances Lincoln, 2006.

Dormandy, Thomas. *The White Death: A History of Tuberculosis*. London: Hambledon and London, 2001.

Gaskell, Elizabeth. *Life of Charlotte Brontë*. London: Dent, 1971.

Green, Dudley. *Patrick Brontë: Father of Genius*. Briscombe Port, Stroud: Nonsuch Publishing, 2008.

Helm, W.H. "Tuberculosis and the Brontë Family." *Brontë Studies* volume 27, July 2002.

Inman, Laura. "'The Awful Event' in *Wuthering Heights*." *Brontë Studies* volume 33, part 3 (November 2008).

Keats, John. *The Complete Poems of John Keats*. New York: Modern 2003.

Keats, John. *The Letters of John Keats*. Edited by H. Buxton Forman. www.elibron.com: Elibron Classics, 2005.

Lonoff, Sue. *The Belgian Essays*. New Haven: Yale University Press, 1996.

MacCarthy, Fiona. *Byron: Life and Legend*. New York: Farrar, Straus and Giroux, 2002.

Sanger, Charles Percy. "Chronology of *Wuthering Heights*." Appendix to *Structure of Wuthering Heights*. London: Hogarth Press, 1926. Reprinted in *The Authorship and the Structure of Wuthering Heights*. London: Dawsons of Pall Mall, 1967.